You Lead: Step Up!

Gary D. Ball

Copyright 2017 Gary D. Ball

All Scripture quotations unless otherwise designated are from the Holy Bible, New International Version. Copyright 1973, 1978, 1984 by International Bible Society. Used by permission of Zondervan Publishing House. All rights reserved.

Permission to quote from the following additional copyrighted versions of Scripture is acknowledged with appreciation:

Scripture quotations marked KJV are from the King James Version.

Cover Design and Graphics by Lacey Bowles Ball

Editorial Services provided by David Yeazell
dayeazell@juno.com
All rights reserved.

ISBN-13: 978-1539472742
ISBN-10: 1539472744

DEDICATION

I dedicate this book to the Lord, the Faithful One. You are faithful to everyone You create from before their birth through Your eternity. I am a witness that You are faithful to love, lead, rescue, guide, provide, protect, teach, heal, free, and inspire. Whatever we need, we can count on You.

I dedicate this book to my parents, Dallas and Faye Ball. I sincerely appreciate your love and faithful leadership in our family, church, and community. I want to be like you when I grow up.

CONTENTS

Acknowledgments

Introduction ... 1

1. Leaders Love ... 7
2. Leaders Listen ... 17
3. Leaders Have Vision ... 27
4. Leaders Aim High ... 41
5. Leaders Serve ... 47
6. Leaders Desire Purity ... 53
7. Leaders Seek Wisdom ... 61
8. Leaders Fail ... 67
9. Leaders Confront Opposition ... 75
10. Leaders Resolve Conflict ... 85
11. Leaders Equip Others ... 93
12. Leaders Make A Difference ... 101

About the Author

ACKNOWLEDGMENTS

Prophet Jim Reilly for listening intently to the voice of God and boldly sharing His word inspiring me to write this book. Thank you!

The people in the communities where I have lived in Kentucky and North Carolina, and the churches and ministries I have served who have been used by God to patiently and graciously enable me to grow as a leader. I owe all of you an enormous debt of gratitude: Boylston Baptist Church, St. Luke United Methodist Church, Walker Memorial UMC, Wesley Manor Retirement Home, Hopkinsville First UMC, Lewisburg UMC, Epley UMC, Concord UMC, Masonville UMC, Utica UMC, Glasgow UMC, the seventy-five churches of the Madisonville District of the United Methodist Church, Crestwood UMC, Main Street Prayer Center, Victory Church, Grace Fellowship, Christview Fellowship and Rapha House.

My faithful prayer partners as I wrote this book: Joel Ball, Marcia Ball, JoAnn Borum, Lois Clayton, Jean Drzewiecki, Sherry Hobgood, Greg Lewis, Jan Medford, Jeff Medford, Philip McCoy, Suzanne Pagano, Connie Peden, Greg Ranes, Barry Sutton, and Cindy Sutton. Thank you for every time you faithfully interceded on my behalf.

David Yeazell for your loyal friendship and encouragement as I wrote. Thank you for your insightful editing to enhance the flow of our book.

Lacey Ball for using your artistic gifts to create the book cover.

Marcia Ball for your faithful encouragement over many months to write. You are an amazing gift of God to me.

INTRODUCTION

You lead. To someone, somewhere you are a leader. Step up! Lead! You and I make a difference in the lives of the persons we lead. We enable adverse change, or we help affect positive transformation in someone's life.

Everyone is a leader to someone. You lead in your marriage and family. As a parent, you lead your children at home. You are a leader at work or school. You lead your siblings. You lead in your church or community. You may well be a leader wherever you go.

You may know with certainty you are a gifted leader, or you may believe you have little or nothing to offer anyone. Either way, you can be certain someone, somewhere is watching you closely. You lead.

It has been said, "If you want to know if you are truly a leader, look behind you to see if anyone is following you." Who is watching you? Who is walking in your footsteps? What road are you traveling? Do you want others to follow where you are going?

The inspiration to write this book came from God. This assurance came to me in worship at my home church, Rapha House in Mills River, North Carolina. Jake Hornaday, a minister with Global Legacy and guest speaker for the evening, began his teaching session by leading us in a directed experience with God. When he instructed us to close our eyes and use our spiritual imaginations, I immediately had an incredible vision.

"Can you see Jesus?" he asked.

In my spirit, I suddenly envisioned myself standing in front of Jesus.

"He has a gift for you."

In the vision, Jesus stood with His right hand slightly hidden behind His robe concealing something. I held out my hands, prepared to receive the surprise gift. His hands lifted from behind his robe to reveal a book.

I was in the early stages of writing our (God's, mine, and many people who prayed and helped) first book, *A Life of Prayer: Step Closer to God*. When the book Jesus held in His hand came into my view, the bright, multicolored cover came alive. Radiant colors leaped off the front cover into the air. He opened the book, and a beam of light shot into the sky. I knew then the book I was currently writing was an amazing gift from Jesus!

"Jesus wants to take you to the Father," Jake directed.

The vision continued as Jesus took me by the hand to lead me into a beautiful mansion where I saw Father God. Peace and a sense of excitement accompanied the warm hospitality I experienced in His presence.

As we stood in a spacious, very magnificent room I heard Jake's direction, "Father God has a gift for you, too." To my surprise, He held a different book in His hand. I don't remember anything specific from the vision about this book, but I was overwhelmed by the gift of a second book I believed would be divinely inspired.

Convinced God wanted me to write a second book; I patiently waited for Him to reveal to me the subject and the contents. On March 13, 2016, God spoke to me through Jim Reilly's prophetic declaration that I was to write a book about leadership. That subject surprised me because I believed I had nothing new, profound or exciting to write about leadership.

These are the words he spoke to me that evening precisely as he gave them:

> By the way, you're supposed to write a book. It is about time you did. (I told him, "I have already written one.") Huh! You've got to write another one. You've got to write one more. Let me tell you what you've got to write on. God's going to give you insight.
>
> He wants you to write on leadership. I've given you unusual ability and insight on leadership. You've got the model of servanthood because you are a servant. You did that your whole life.
>
> Nobody's written a model on leadership. They've taken the world's systems on leadership, and that's what they've given. If you do this I will give it worldwide. Because I need people to understand who I am.
>
> And God has had to take you to places that none of us have ever been. Brother, you're a leader in so many ways. That's what God thinks about you, because everywhere you go you serve, even when you were a district guy you served. You said, "I'll do it if I can serve." That's what you did.
>
> He said, "If you will write this book on leadership ... It won't be a thick book, but it's going to be a book that will go worldwide. And it will literally change cultures.

After hearing this prophetic word, I began soon afterward to write.

I am sure you have already surmised, I write this book from a Christian perspective. It is my deepest desire to hear God's revelation of real

Christian leadership. I asked Him for His words every time I sat down to write, and my prayer partners joined me requesting His divine insight.

I am a Leader

I have been in positions of leadership throughout my life. I initially learned to lead in my family church, and as a pre-teen in the Boy Scout troop. In church, I began leading as an usher during Sunday evening worship. I learned to lead public prayer when requested. A sense of belonging in the church gave me the confidence to share my faith and contribute to life in the community even in those early years.

In our Boy Scout troop, I worked diligently to advance in the ranks. Our adult leaders and my peers soon invited me to take leadership responsibilities. I helped lead our meetings, plan our outdoor activities and challenge the younger boys to apply themselves to move to the next level of Scouting.

I believe God is always preparing us in each successive season of life for our future leadership assignments. As I look back on my life, I see how He equipped me as a child and teenager to serve later in leadership as a pastor.

One of the ways He prepared me was to open the door for my first job. I worked part-time as a high school student at a country store and gas station just down the road from our home. I usually walked the quarter mile to the Longview Store every afternoon after school and on Saturdays.

Although I was unaware of it at the time, God began then to teach me how to relate to people with respect, affirming their dignity and worth. Customers from all walks of life came to shop at the little country store. Each one had a unique personality and way of thinking. Some were always pleasant with happy smiles on their faces. They were never hard to please. Others were rather grumpy with either a stern look or a frown on their faces. I learned the value of assisting everyone in a friendly, professional manner with little regard for their current disposition.

In college, I was a part of the leadership team of the Baptist Student Union at Western Carolina University my sophomore year. I served in leadership on the Student Ministry Team at Gardner-Webb College my junior and senior years. I never desired any of those positions of leadership. I never felt worthy or adequately equipped to fulfill the responsibilities. I always believed someone else could do it better. I would much rather have kept my back-row seat. I didn't see myself as a leader, though others apparently did.

As a student at Southern Baptist Theological Seminary, I began serving in my first paid leadership position in the church in 1975 as youth pastor of Saint Luke United Methodist Church in Louisville, Kentucky. From that time on I served throughout my adult life as a pastor of local churches. Even though I recognized I was leading churches, I did not readily identify myself as a "leader."

Changing My Perceptions

In 1997, I was called by God and appointed to serve as pastor of Glasgow First United Methodist Church in Kentucky. While living in Glasgow, several experiences caused my perception of my leadership to begin to change. During the first three summer months, my district superintendent, Wallace Thomas, began encouraging all the pastors in our district to read Rick Warren's book, *The Purpose Driven Church*. I bought the book after the third time he recommended it and couldn't put it down.

God's vision and strategy for ministry with this congregation came clearly into focus as I read. I understood the purpose of the church more clearly than ever. I had a firmer grasp than ever before on how to lead the church to fulfill its mission. I longed to be more intentional. My deepest desire was to produce more fruit for the Kingdom of God. God had called me and was guiding me to lead this church.

A few weeks after reading the book I had the opportunity to participate in a Purpose Driven Church Conference at the Saddleback Community Church in Lake Forest, California. During one of the worship sessions, I knelt at the altar and promised God, "No more business as usual."

Previously the leadership and I had most often decided what we thought was best for the church to do and asked God to bless it. But, I promised God I would change. I determined we would listen to God to learn what He was doing and join Him. I was confident this approach would produce much more fruit.

God began to bring many new people into the life of Glasgow First United Methodist Church. Worship attendance increased, requiring the church to start a second worship service or build a new sanctuary. We decided to start a contemporary worship service.

It was soon after we successfully began the second worship experience that my friend and fellow pastor, John Shepherd asked me, "Do you realize the other pastors in our county are watching what you are doing?" God used John's question to transform my attitude and understanding of my leadership. For the first time, I began to recognize and identify myself as a leader. I fully accepted the gift and position of leadership God had graciously given to me.

Since that time, my heart overflows with gratitude to God who chose to give me this gift I know I don't deserve. I decided to very intentionally live my life and serve God using the gift of leadership to the best of my ability. I have attempted to polish the gift of leadership by attending conferences on leadership, reading books on the subject, and carefully observing the lives of the leaders I respect.

I began to identify myself as a leader over the next three years. God gave me new insights, new determination, and new strategies for pastoral leadership with the Glasgow church. God called me to a new level of leadership in the community as pastors began to pray together and to work in ministry together to bring revival and transformation to our city. They asked me to serve as leader of the group. I knew I had the best handle on what it meant to lead as a pastor than I had ever experienced.

Then God called me to yet another level of leadership. James King, bishop of the Kentucky Area of the United Methodist Church asked me to serve as the Madisonville District Superintendent. I had just finally begun to understand and identify myself as a leader. I had the best understanding of what it meant to lead as a pastor and had started to produce more fruit in ministry than ever.

As I explained more fully in our first book, *A Life of Prayer: Step Closer to God*, I didn't feel qualified to fulfill the responsibilities of a district superintendent. I felt I had just become comfortable with my new identity as a leader. I did not want to leave Glasgow where God was moving so powerfully to bring people into His Kingdom. But, God's call was crystal clear to me. I surrendered to what I earnestly believed was His will and plan for my life.

Just as I had become most comfortable leading as pastor of a church, God graciously invited me to leave my comfort zone to take me to a new place. He wanted me to lead as a pastor to pastors. He began to reveal how He wanted me to focus my efforts and energies on spiritual leadership.

Becoming a Spiritual Leader

I now knew I was a leader, but His desire for my life involved focusing more narrowly on being a "spiritual leader." He began to show me the difference between leadership and spiritual leadership. Although the responsibilities of district superintendent included administrative duties, He did not want me to be an efficient administrator or a competent chief executive officer. I was to focus on spiritual leadership as an entrepreneurial shepherd.

He reminded me of His promise, "But seek first His kingdom and His righteousness, and all these things will be given to you as well" (Matt. 6:33). When I focused on my relationship with Him and led the pastors I shepherded to do the same; all the other things fell in line. God took care of all the other concerns in my ministry: pastoral leaders for the churches, starting new ministries, planting a new church, financial needs, legal matters—everything. Faithful to His promise, He provided much more than we could ever have imagined!

I soon understood in a new way that one of the spiritual gifts God offers is the gift of leadership. In Romans 12:6-8 the Apostle Paul writes:

We have different gifts, according to the grace given us. If a man's gift is prophesying, let him use it in proportion to his faith. If it is serving, let him serve; if it is teaching, let him teach; if it is to encouraging, let him encourage; if it is contributing to the needs of others, let him give generously; <u>if it is leadership, let him govern diligently</u>; if it is showing mercy, let him do it cheerfully. (emphasis mine).

I lead. My heart's desire is to lead diligently. I want to please God. I want to partner with Him to enable people to live abundant, fruitful lives in the Kingdom of God.

You lead. I hope you are a spiritual leader. It is my hope and prayer that this book will help equip you to lead diligently.

CHAPTER 1: LEADERS LOVE

We love God with all our heart, soul, mind, and strength, and we love others as we love ourselves with the love of God. God is the source of and creates and initiates all true love. Whether we acknowledge Him or not, He instills all love into the hearts of every human He created. We were all formed in His image with the capacity to love.

God's very nature is love. He is forever demonstrating His love for us in ways we understand and celebrate and in ways we cannot comprehend with our finite human minds. His love for us is unconditional—no strings attached. We love Him because He loved us first and gave us the ability to love Him with our whole being.

> This is how God showed His love among us: He sent His one and only Son into the world that we might live through Him. This is love: not that we loved God, but that He loved us and sent His Son as an atoning sacrifice for our sins. (1 Jn. 4:9-10)

Leaders Love God

We set our sights on perfect love. God loves perfectly and unconditionally. Jesus is the supreme example of a leader who loves. He cares about all our needs, even the simplest ones. He always compassionately moves to fulfill our physical, emotional, relational and spiritual needs.

God loves us and invites us to love Him in response. When we love God first, and above everything else, we experience unspeakable joy and peace that passes understanding. "But seek first His kingdom and His righteousness, and all these things will be given to you as well" (Matt. 6:33).

The constant worries of life disappear when we seek a personal, intimate relationship with God. When we make our relationship with God the first and last order of the day, we have no need to worry.

We express our love for God in unique and tangible ways. We convey our love for Him when we communicate with Him through prayer—the most basic and simple way every human being can express love for our Creator. He is always patiently waiting for us to share our joys, sorrows, needs, trust, trials, and faith with Him. This intimate time with Almighty God is the foundational way we reveal our love for Him. Our entire relationship with Him is built on this cornerstone.

We express our love for God when we worship. Worship, in its most basic form, is simply our expression of love to God. We do this as we sing, pray, read and listen to His Word, and offer our spiritual and financial gifts.

Much of modern worship is singing about God. I believe worship in its truest form is singing to Him. Many of the most popular hymns and contemporary worship songs are those we sing directly to God—hymns that touch the core of our being: "How Great Thou Art," "Holy, Holy, Holy, Lord God Almighty" and "My Jesus, I Love Thee." We sing contemporary songs addressed directly to our Lord: "10,000 Reasons (Bless the Lord)" by Matt Redmon, "No Longer Slaves" by Jonathan David and Melissa Helser, "Your Grace Is Enough" by Chris Tomlin, "Good, Good Father" by Chris Tomlin or "Great Are You Lord" by Casting Crowns.

I believe our most powerful expression of love for God is obedience. Jesus declared, "If you love me, you will obey what I command" (Jn. 14:15). If we love Him, our desire is to please Him. Trust is at the core of true love. When we do what He asks, we are expressing our trust in who He is and His plan for our lives. God promises in Deuteronomy 5:10 to show love to a thousand future generations of those who love and obey Him now.

Leaders Love Others

Love originates with God. "We love because He first loved us" (1 Jn. 4:19). God is the ultimate source of all love, and He plants all the love we have for others in our hearts. Since God is love (1 Jn. 4:16), our love for others increases and intensifies when we accept the gift of God's love into our lives.

"Dear friends, since God so loved us, we also ought to love one another. No one has ever seen God; but if we love one another, God lives in us and His love is made complete in us" (1 Jn. 4:11-12).

We encounter people throughout our lives whom we find difficult to love. Sometimes the difficulty we experience in failing to love someone stems from an issue in our lives. The difficult person may push a button that brings those issues to the forefront. At other times, the persons we find difficult to love may have serious problems and personal issues. Their actions and decisions bring conflict, confusion, and dysfunction to their lives and to others we lead. Often these persons are a part of our immediate family, friends, and sphere of influence where we are forced to interact with them frequently.

God invites and challenges us to love everyone the way He loves them. Failure to demonstrate love to those we find difficult to love may well be one of the greatest hindrances to successful leadership we will encounter. "This is how we know what love is: Jesus Christ laid down his life for us. And we ought to lay down our lives for our brothers" (1 Jn. 3:16). True love is evident when we set aside our issues and personal desires for the sake of others. Are you laying down your life so others can have life?

I am continually amazed by the loving example of our prayer team in His Presence Healing Rooms. As director of this prayer ministry, I have the privilege to witness our team members demonstrate love to people who are difficult to love. Our team does not give up or give out when people come for prayer time after time with no apparent change in their lives. We know God is working, but they sometimes reject His love and direction. It is very tough to continue to love them and pray again with them. But, our team, without exception or hesitation, loves them faithfully.

Leaders Love Family

Our love of others begins with love for our family. My goal as a Christian leader is to love God and give Him first place in my life. My second priority is the demonstration of the love I feel in my heart for my family. A close, deep and intimate relationship with my wife is at the top of that list. I want to know her and be known by her at the deepest levels of life. It is my deep longing to relate to her as my closest friend.

Most often, I have been able to keep my priorities in order. But, at times I have fallen far short of the mark. I failed most frequently when my work in the church took precedence over my marriage and family. When that happened, usually a concern in someone else's life overshadowed my relationship with my wife and children, as I mistakenly chose my work in the church over them. No one comes to the close of their work or ministry and says, "I wish I had spent more time at work." Instead, we are much more likely to lament, "I wish I had spent more time with my family."

The most meaningful and fulfilling way I express love to my family is to spend quality time with them. There were frequent crises in the church requiring my immediate pastoral attention: illnesses resulting in hospitalization, death, and marriage conflicts. To ensure the best quality time with my family, I learned to schedule a day off each week. We usually spent the entire day together as a family. All of us appreciated most the times we could get away from the phone calls, the daily chores, or people dropping by our home. Our most memorable experiences are of day trips to the park, picnicking, camping, bike riding, or playing ball in the backyard.

Years later, I discovered the need to view each day in blocks of time. Since the responsibilities of pastoral ministry required frequent evenings away from home, I learned to identify blocks of time in the morning or afternoon to spend with family. This approach afforded me the opportunity to give them more quality time as an expression of my love for them.

Early in my ministry, God revealed the need to take vacation time with family. I was always thankful for the way God guided and moved on the hearts of leaders in the churches to make vacation time possible. Most of our vacations were week-long visits with our families in North Carolina. We experienced the love of parents, siblings, and their families. Our time together refreshed us so we were ready to give ourselves anew to the work to which the Lord called us.

Don't neglect to express your love for your family. Minister to their needs first. Paul writes in 1 Timothy 3:4-5 these instructions to Timothy giving the qualifications of leaders: "He must manage his own family well and see that his children obey him, and he must do so in a manner worthy of full respect. (If anyone does not know how to manage his own family, how can he take care of God's church?)"

Faithfully and diligently express love to your spouse and family. Do not neglect them in the name of ministry.

Love in Word

If you sincerely love the people you lead, express your love in words. People everywhere appreciate hearing the affirmation, "I love you" when it is shared by someone whom they perceive is speaking truthfully from the heart. It is of vital importance for leaders to learn this lesson.

Show your love when the people you lead gather corporately. Express your love personally to the individuals you serve. Do this appropriately, so you are not misunderstood.

Gary Chapman has written several excellent books on the topic of expressing love. I highly recommend his book, *The Five Love Languages: How to Express Heartfelt Commitment to Your Mate*. His premise surmised from serving many years as a pastor and Christian marriage counselor is that every human receives and shows love in unique ways.

Gary Chapman contends that we all have one or more primary love languages. We experience love through words of affirmation, quality time, receiving gifts, acts of service, and physical touch.

Love Encourages

One of the greatest mistakes leaders today frequently make is failing to affirm the people on their teams in their work or ministry. We often earnestly appreciate the people with whom we work, but fail to tell them. Employees frequently bemoan, "No one appreciates me for the work I do. I am diligent and faithful, but no one ever says, 'Thank you!' I never hear our leadership say, 'Good job!' We are expected to do our work without any encouragement from our leaders." Through words of affirmation, express your appreciation frequently.

I believe every person God created appreciates and yearns for encouragement. Christian leaders understand the admonition from God, "Therefore encourage one another and build each other up, just as in fact you are doing" (1 Thess. 5:11). We recognize the command, "But encourage one another daily…" (Heb. 3:13).

Our Creator formed our minds and hearts to require encouragement. He reminds us in His love letter (the Bible) to offer words of affirmation to one another every day.

Many people suffer verbal abuse in their homes and workplaces. Few people experience significant encouragement throughout their lives. Many people are starving for encouragement. It has been my personal experience that even a little encouragement goes a long way toward helping people reach their potential. Imagine what an incredible difference it would make in our lives if we were being encouraged every day.

Anyone whose primary love language is words of affirmation will thrive as they experience encouragement. If they don't frequently hear words of affirmation, they don't feel loved and appreciated. It has been my personal experience that these persons often work very hard and make a definite difference in the lives of others but frequently find it difficult to believe people think so highly of them. The truth is, they simply need to hear our words of affirmation and encouragement regularly.

Love in Deed

It is not sufficient to express our love in words only. People need to experience our love in other tangible ways. Your leadership quotient will rise among those you serve if you spend quality time with them. People desire your undivided attention where your focus is entirely on them. Quality time is my primary love language. I feel a person's love most readily when they are willing to give their time to our relationship. Spending time face to face with others is the primary tangible way I express love best. I want quality time with my wife and family as often as possible.

Many people experience love most readily when they receive a gift. They respond to visual expressions of love and appreciation. Gift giving is taken very seriously and given much thought and time. Gift givers always seem to offer the perfect gift—carefully selected and given out of a personal relationship with the receiver.

Others relate best to acts of service. Taking the time to plan and carry out even simple acts of service requires effort and energy. If a person's primary love language is acts of service, they appreciate any gesture of our help in practical ways.

Your appropriate physical touch is an expression of love, especially to those persons whose primary love language is physical touch. Laying your hand gently on their arm or shoulder speaks volumes to them. A kiss expresses love without words to your child, spouse or parent. When you warmly embrace a friend or family member you are actively demonstrating your love.

It is a vital leadership principle to listen and observe carefully those we lead discerning their primary love languages. We learn which love language they understand best, and we then communicate our love and appreciation for them using that specific love language whenever possible.

Love Sacrifices

The greatest expression of love in all of history was the suffering and death of God's own Son. Jesus willingly offered His life for the sake of ours. Leaders are called to follow His example. "Then He said to them all: 'If anyone would come after Me, he must deny himself and take up his cross daily and follow Me. For whoever wants to save his life will lose it, but whoever loses his life for Me will save it'". (Lk. 9:23-24)

Sin contradicts love. The root of sin is the single letter "I" in the middle of the word. When we fail to deny ourselves, we sin. Jesus calls His followers to deny themselves daily. Leaders forsake their desires to meet the needs of others. Genuine expressions of love require small or great acts of self-denial every day. Love sacrifices for the sake of others. When we follow our Leader, we die to selfish ambition as we take up our cross daily to go with Him. We find abundant life as we abandon our lives to the love of Jesus and of others.

Love Forgives

People you lead will make mistakes. You will be hurt and offended at times. Sometimes, their mistakes will feel very personal to you. Learn to forgive. Ask God every time you are hurt or offended to empower you to forgive.

The ability to forgive is supernatural. As human beings, we were all created by God with the capacity to forgive. But, it is not our inclination to forgive others when we are offended by their words or actions.

We never fully understand nor practice forgiveness until we have first fully experienced the forgiveness of God. We forgive because God forgave us first. The personal experience of being forgiven by God frees us to forgive others. God expects us to forgive because He forgives us. Our Father forgives all sins we commit against Him and others (see Ps. 103:3). He equips us to do the same. It is only by His power we are capable of such forgiveness.

In Mark 11:25 Jesus instructs us, "And when you stand praying, if you hold anything against anyone, forgive them, so that your Father in heaven may forgive you your sins." There is no room in the Kingdom of God for unforgiveness. We are to forgive anyone anything they have done to hurt or offend us. This is not an easy task, but, it is possible, or the Lord would not ask us to do so.

Give people who have failed a second chance. Don't write them off the first time they don't fulfill your expectations, hurt you, or fail you. Don't write them off the second or third time they hurt or fail you. Learn to forgive as many as seventy-seven times (see Matt. 18:21-22).

Sow Love

"Do not be deceived: God cannot be mocked. A man reaps what he sows" (Gal. 6:7). I am very thankful God fills my heart with love for others. God is the Source of the gift of love and compassion we have in our hearts for others. I can give witness to this truth: if we sow love, we reap love in return.

Throughout my life, God has sent my family and me to communities to live and to serve in ministry where people were easy to love. There were only a few rare exceptions of persons who were difficult to love.

Coming from a home filled with Christian love I experienced abundant love all my life. I was accepted and encouraged by my parents and three brothers. Our home church was full of people who loved and obeyed God. Pastors, teachers, neighbors, and friends sowed abundant love into my life.

I began to understand and accept the love God poured out on me at an early age. All this made it easy to sow my love and the love of God into the lives of the people in the churches and communities where He sent us to live. In return, I reaped love. I am often overwhelmed by our family's harvest of love.

I began serving as associate pastor of the Hopkinsville First United Methodist Church in June 1982. Both Marcia and I immediately loved the community and the people in the church. We did not have difficulty sowing our love and the love of God into their lives.

We were expecting our third son, Joel, less than a year after moving to Hopkinsville. Marcia began experiencing complications with the pregnancy and the doctor prescribed complete bed rest. He instructed her to only get up to go to the bathroom. This made for a challenging situation since our oldest son Manuel was three years old and Aaron was only one and a half. We desperately needed help!

We soon began to reap love from the church. The leadership of the church wanted me to be able to continue to serve in ministry, but knew I could not care for our two sons and work at the same time. A Sunday school class for young adults with children took the lead. At first, they intended to take turns providing childcare for us but decided the daily changes would be too difficult for our sons. They decided to donate enough money to provide child care. We found a loving young woman to care for the boys every morning while I worked. The gift was so large we paid her twice the going rate and had money left over.

We reaped more and more love. The Sunday school class began providing a meal every day for our family. After only a few days our refrigerator was overflowing. When we requested they bring meals every other day, we still had more delicious food than we could eat.

We learned our babysitter was a Christian but did not have a church home. Her military husband was not a Christian. Our families developed a relationship of love and trust. Within a few weeks, her husband gave his heart to Jesus, and both became faithful members of the church. We all reaped great outpourings of the love of God!

Love Is Faithful

One of the unique characteristics of a spiritual leader is faithfulness. God searches the hearts and lives of leaders for faithfulness. God is always faithful, and He created us to be like Him. God is faithful to keep every promise He makes (see Heb. 10:23 and 1 Thess. 5:24). From before we were born and into eternity He is forever revealing His faithfulness to us.

He promises if we are faithful in the little things He will place us in leadership positions with greater responsibility. "His master replied, 'Well done, good and faithful servant! You have been faithful with a few things; I will put you in charge of many things. Come and share your master's happiness!'" (Matt. 25:21).

This is one of the most exciting and challenging spiritual principles established by God from the beginning. You will know He considers you a faithful servant when He gives you increased responsibility.

Having experienced the fulfillment of this spiritual principle several times in my life, I have been surprised and challenged every time God gave me greater responsibility as a leader. One of my most memorable moments occurred when I served as pastor of the Masonville and Utica United Methodist Churches, two rural congregations near Owensboro, Kentucky for five years.

One February day near the end of the five years, Marcia and I heard God speak the same words while separately studying Henry Blackaby and Claude King's *Experiencing God*. We both knew God was preparing our hearts to move to serve another church when we read the words, "You cannot go with God and stay where you are."

Two months later we learned God was sending us to Glasgow First United Methodist Church, placing me in charge of a congregation twice the combined size of the two churches I was currently serving. I would be challenged to lead the new church with a staff and significantly more ministries to oversee. I was both amazed and humbled that God trusted me to lead this church.

Dr. Glenn Sowards, my District Superintendent in Owensboro, encouraged and challenged me, "Gary you have been a faithful pastor to the people here. You can do the same thing in the new church. You will just need to do things in a shorter amount of time."

God has taught me the power of faithfulness through my parents. Mom and Dad consistently modeled faithfulness my entire life. They were faithful to one another in marriage in sickness and in health for more than sixty-five years until my mother's death. They were faithful disciples of Jesus from the time they were saved and entered a covenant relationship with Him. They consistently lived what they believed and taught.

My parents were loyal to the church all their lives. Mom was a dedicated leader, serving well into her eighties as a youth Sunday school teacher. She led faithfully as church treasurer for many years. Dad served as a deacon for over fifty years.

Our parents faithfully led our family, now three generations deep beyond them. We never doubted or questioned their love for us. Spiritual leadership is at the core of the way they demonstrated love. They prepared us for life by taking us to worship and fellowship in the church every time there was an opportunity. Before we could read, they began reading Bible stories to my brothers and me to teach us truth and spiritual principles. They modeled pure, holy lives as they followed the Master.

A spiritual leader is faithful to love. "Let love and faithfulness never leave you; bind them around your neck, write them on the tablet of your heart. Then you will win favor and a good name in the sight of God and man" (Prov. 3:3-4).

Love is Indispensable

The Apostle Paul speaks in his first letter to the Corinthian church about spiritual gifts (1 Cor. 12). He then wrote these words, "And now I will show you the most excellent way" (1 Cor. 12:31) and follows in 1 Corinthians 13 with undeniably the greatest description of true love known to man.

> If I speak in the tongues of men and of angels, but have not love, I am only a resounding gong or a clanging cymbal. If I have the gift of prophecy and can fathom all mysteries and all knowledge, and if I have a faith that can move mountains, but have not love, I am nothing. If I give all I possess to the poor and surrender my body to the flames, but have not love, I gain nothing. Love is patient, love is kind. It does not envy, it does not boast, it is not proud. It is not rude, it is not self-seeking, it is not easily angered, it keeps no record

of wrongs. Love does not delight in evil but rejoices with the truth. It always protects, always trusts, always hopes, always perseveres. Love never fails. But where there are prophecies, they will cease; where there are tongues, they will be stilled; where there is knowledge, it will pass away. For we know in part and we prophesy in part, but when perfection comes, the imperfect disappears. When I was a child, I talked like a child, I thought like a child, I reasoned like a child. When I became a man, I put childish ways behind me. Now we see but a poor reflection as in a mirror; then we shall see face to face. Now I know in part; then I shall know fully, even as I am fully known. And now these three remain: faith, hope and love. But the greatest of these is love. (1 Corinthians 13:1-13)

Love is truly the most excellent way; it is indispensable. Fruitful spiritual leaders will embody unconditional love described in this biblical passage.

Ask God to examine your heart as a leader. Is your heart filled with love for Him and for others? As you read the description of the ultimate expression of love in 1 Corinthians 13, where do you fall short? How would others evaluate your expression of love for them in view of 1 Corinthians 13? Without love, nothing counts.

You lead. Step up to love God and others!

CHAPTER 2: LEADERS LISTEN

If you love, you listen. Listening to others is a tangible expression of love. Christian leaders want always to improve their ability to listen well. It is vital that we learn to discern and carefully listen to the voice of God. We also need to learn to hear what the people we lead are saying.

Learn to Listen to God

God listens to us when we speak to Him in prayer. He yearns for us to hear Him when He speaks. Effective spiritual leaders learn to actively listen to the voice of God. It was Jesus who declared authoritatively, "My sheep listen to my voice; I know them, and they follow me" (Jn. 10:27).

Learning to hear God is extremely vital for spiritual leaders. "He said, 'If you listen carefully to the Lord your God and do what is right in His eyes, if you pay attention to His commands and keep all His decrees, I will not bring on you any of the diseases I brought on the Egyptians, for I am the Lord, who heals you'" (Ex. 15:26). Listening must be coupled with obedience to do what the Lord tells us to do.

As a parent have you ever exclaimed to your child, "You are not listening to me!"? Maybe as a spouse, you have uttered in desperation, "You never listen to what I say!" What we ultimately mean by those words is the person may have heard the words we spoke, but their behavior has not changed. Our child understands but does not obey.

In Isaiah 55:2-3 the Lord outlines His rewards when we listen to Him,

> Why spend money on what is not bread,
>   and your labor on what does not satisfy?
> Listen, listen to Me, and eat what is good,
>   and your soul will delight in the richest of fare.
> Give ear and come to Me;
>   hear Me, that your soul may live.

I will make an everlasting covenant with you,
  My faithful love promised to David.

Listening to God is essential for strong spiritual leadership. Do the people you lead recognize you as one who walks and talks with God? Do you know His voice? Do you enjoy an intimate relationship with the Lord? Do you model listening and obeying His voice for those you lead?

Listen When God Calls

The Bible records many accounts of God calling ordinary people to lead in a way that altered history. These regular folks were shocked by God's call on their lives to lead. Most were very reluctant to do what they were asked to do because they felt inadequate and poorly prepared for the task. They sometimes suggested God find someone better qualified. Most often their initial reaction was centered in the fact that they believed it all depended on their willingness and abilities. The truth is, it was God's vision, and He desired to fulfill it with their help.

Moses was an ordinary person with an unusual background. He was born to Hebrew parents who trusted the one true God. Yet, he was raised in the palace of a great emperor like a grandson. He was educated as royalty.

His birth mother nursed him and must have passed on her faith to him. At forty years old, Moses killed an Egyptian taskmaster who was mistreating a Hebrew slave. He lived the next forty years as a fugitive in a foreign land. He settled into the ordinary life of a shepherd.

God called Moses to lead the enslaved Hebrew people to freedom. Moses did not view himself as a leader. He challenged God's call because he feared for his life if he returned to Egypt. He did not feel capable or qualified to speak to Pharaoh or the Hebrew leaders.

God's view of Moses was radically different from the picture Moses saw when he looked in the mirror. God trusted Moses to lead His people. The Lord could see the protection and favor He would pour out on Moses and the Israelites. God knew the words He would use to fill the mouth of Moses.

The Lord had already prepared the heart of Moses' brother, Aaron to walk alongside Moses. Moses would not be alone. God promised to go with him, giving him the power to accomplish his mission as a leader. Moses listened and obeyed God's call.

Nehemiah was an ordinary person in a royal position. He served as a servant in the palace as the king's cupbearer. Day after day he faithfully fulfilled his duty to serve the king the finest wine and to protect the king from poisoning. One day he heard the call of God to lead.

The call came through the report of fellow Israelites concerning the deplorable conditions of Nehemiah's people and his native city of Jerusalem. Nehemiah's heart stirred with compassion and grief. He was moved to seek the Lord's help to rebuild his native land beginning with Jerusalem. He confessed his own failure and the failure of his forefathers to obey the Lord. From that point forward God gave Nehemiah favor to accomplish His mission in record-breaking time. Nehemiah's extraordinary leadership was evident as opposition mounted against him and his people. Nehemiah listened and obeyed God's call.

Many other stories of ordinary people who answered God's call are recorded in the pages of the Bible. David, a lowly shepherd, was called by God to lead a nation as king. Gideon, an ordinary farmer, was called by God to captain the armies of his people to defeat an oppressive enemy. Peter, an ordinary fisherman, followed Jesus to become a key leader in the creation of His church. None of these people had ever done anything like what God called them to do. Their call was to partner with God to accomplish what appeared impossible to them.

As disciples (students) of Christ, we model for others a personal relationship with Him which involves more listening than speaking. When we hear His voice, we obey immediately. I have a deep appreciation for the experience of Abraham when God tested his faith and willingness to trust. Abraham knew God's voice the moment he heard Him call his name. He was determined to obey the Lord no matter the cost. "Early the next morning Abraham got up and loaded his donkey. He took with him two of his servants and his son Isaac. When he had cut enough wood for the burnt offering, he set out for the place God had told him about" (Gen. 22:3).

Abraham did not question, argue, or delay. He immediately followed the Lord's instructions.

Are you learning to listen to God's voice? Have you answered His call on your life? Are you fulfilling the destiny God has envisioned for you? Are you resisting God's call today because you feel your failures have disqualified you? Are you ready and willing to answer God's call immediately without reservation or hesitation?

Do Not Listen to satan

In today's world, if a person admits they hear voices in their head they are often considered by professionals and others to be mentally unstable. I have a different opinion. I believe we all hear voices in our heads. I readily admit I consistently hear three voices: my own, God's and satan's.

It is my sincere desire always to hear and always obey the voice of God. Sometimes I need to listen carefully to my own inner voice, my God-given conscience, rational thinking, and history of personal experiences. But, I never want to listen to the voice of the enemy, because he always lies.

Jesus warned those who refused to listen to Him and His Father,

"Why is my language not clear to you? Because you are unable to hear what I say. You belong to your father, the devil, and you want to carry out your father's desires. He was a murderer from the beginning, not holding to the truth, for there is no truth in him. When he lies, he speaks his native language, for he is a liar and the father of lies." (John. 8:43-44)

Notice Jesus very emphatically declares, "There is no truth in him." Satan's normal mode of operation is to start with enough truth to set his hooks in us, then end with a bold-faced lie. These half-truths satan spreads are still absolute lies.

Don't listen to the enemy. The only power he has over us is the power we grant him when we believe and accept his lies as truth. He is always a liar! Even the roaring noise he makes as he prowls around seeking someone to devour is a lie (see 1 Pet. 5:8). He has no power except the power produced by our believing the lie that he has power over us.

Satan's power is generated by the fear his lies create. He makes a lot of noise, his voice is very loud, because he demands to be heard. His tactic is to roar loud and long to break down our resistance to his temptations. Do not listen to the voice of the devil.

God is omnipresent. He is present anywhere and everywhere all the time. Many Christians believe the lie that satan is the same. That is a lie! He can only be one place at any given time because he is a created being. God created an angel named lucifer. He rebelled against Almighty God, and he was banished from heaven along with one-third of the angels. Satan cannot tempt everyone at once. He can only send demons to oppress believers or possess unbelievers.

The demons are fallen angels whose only power is the power of the lie. For every demon who does satan's bidding, there are at least two angels who hear and obey the voice of God. The devil and his army of demons are outnumbered at least two to one! Don't listen to the devil! He is lying every single time. No exceptions. Lying is his native language.

Learn to Listen to Others
"The way of fools seems right to them, but the wise listen to advice" (Prov. 12:15). The foolish only listen to their own inner voice. Discernment of truth and direction come when we learn to listen to others. Sometimes the guidance of others is wise and prudent, but at other times it may be destructive. "Let the wise listen and add to their learning, and let the discerning get guidance—for understanding proverbs and parables, the sayings and riddles of the wise" (Prov. 1:5).

As spiritual leaders make decisions, we always consider the

consequences of these decisions on relationships. How will this decision affect my relationship with God? How will it affect my relationship with the special people in my life? How will this decision affect the interpersonal relationships of the people I lead? Listen to the voice of God and your most trusted counselors for guidance.

Sometimes we listen to the counsel of others, and it is wise advice. King Solomon is given the distinction of being the wisest man who ever lived. His wise counsel was apparent early in his reign.

1 Kings 3 tells the story of two mothers seeking justice before King Solomon. The women had each given birth to a son, one born only three days before the other. One of the mothers had accidentally laid on her child in the bed at night, and he died. Both parents claimed the living baby belonged to her. When they argued before him, Solomon gave orders, "Cut the living baby in half with a sword and give half to one and a half to the other."

The barbaric decree of Solomon yielded the truth. The birth mother hastily pled with the king to allow the other woman to take the child rather than kill him. King Solomon wisely awarded the baby to its birth mother. Sometimes we listen to wise counsel and lives are saved and transformed.

Refusal to heed a warning from a wise person can have disastrous results. Acts 27 records the story of the beginning of the Apostle Paul's journey to Rome following his arrest. He was handed over to a Roman centurion to be transported by ship to stand trial. The boisterous winter weather made sailing extremely dangerous. While in Fair Havens, a safe harbor, Paul heard the voice of God and warned the centurion, the ship's owner and its pilot against continuing the voyage. But, they all rejected his advice that would have protected the ship, its cargo and the lives of everyone on board.

Very soon after the ship left the island, a storm of hurricane force struck the ship, forcing the sailors to take drastic measures to save it. All the ship's cargo, tackle, the lifeboat, and anchors were lost during the fourteen-day storm. Finally, pounding surf broke the ship into pieces when it was driven aground on a sand bar off the shore of the Island of Malta.

Just as Paul had warned, all was lost except the lives of the 276 people on board. This tragedy could have been averted if only those in authority had listened to Paul.

Are there times in your life when you refused to listen to the warnings of wise advisors? Recount the ramifications of that experience. What were the consequences?

Listen to Your Parents

We honor our parents when we listen to them throughout our lives. "Listen, my son, to your father's instruction and do not forsake your mother's teaching" (Prov. 1:8).

My parents taught me many life lessons from a Christian perspective. Both lived their lives as faithful, committed believers. One of the life lessons I learned from my father's instruction came while I was a high school student.

As a high school sophomore, I was certain I wanted to get a college education. I'm uncertain how I came to that conclusion since I did not personally know many college graduates. Neither Mom nor Dad had a college background, and neither of them pushed me as the eldest of four sons to attend college. They were both encouraging when I shared my dream with them, but quickly admonished, "We will help you all we can, but with four of you so close together you will need to do all you possibly can."

I began to plan for my future in college by working after school and on weekends. I tithed from my income to the church and spent a little money on things I wanted, but saved almost everything I made for college. Although I frequently dreamed of owning a sports car, I didn't own a vehicle until after I graduated from college.

I researched scholarships and other possibilities for help with college costs. Soon my heart was set on receiving an Army ROTC scholarship while attending North Carolina State University. My dream was to serve four years in the Army as an officer, saving enough money to buy the muscle car of my dreams and build a home I had already begun to design.

When my Dad offered what I later came to realize was wise instruction, at first it felt like he quenched the fire of my dreams. "What if you don't get the Army ROTC Scholarship? You will need a backup plan." His instruction was very realistic and practical. I knew I could not afford the cost of going to the university of my choice without a scholarship. I decided to follow my father's advice and applied to Western Carolina University where the tuition was significantly lower.

My hopes were high that my dreams were about to be fulfilled when invited to a military base for interviews with officers and to undergo a military medical physical. But, near the end of my senior year, I was very disappointed, my hopes and dreams crushed. No scholarship, no NCSU, and no military officer's career. However, I did have a well-developed backup plan.

Within eighteen months I believed with all my heart God Himself had guided the backup plan. He used my experiences at Western Carolina University to direct me into His will as He called me to ministry as a pastor. Today, I still follow the instruction of my father to have a backup plan whenever possible.

Heed the Rebuke of Wise Persons

"It is better to heed a wise man's rebuke than to listen to the song of fools" (Ecc. 7:5). Leaders need people around them who are bold to rebuke whenever necessary. We have people who mentor us formally or informally. We need their encouragement, and the hope and help they bring to our lives. Although rebuke is challenging to receive, we want to give these same persons the permission to speak words of admonition and reproof.

An admonition is always easier to accept from someone we love, trust and know to be wise. Personally, I realize I have not been as open to request or to receive correction as I need to be. Being more open will enable me to grow and improve as a spiritual leader. What about you? Are you receptive to constructive criticism?

There was a time in the life of Moses when constructive criticism transformed his life. During a brief experience in the wilderness with his father-in-law, Jethro, Moses learned a valuable lesson from the rebuke of a wise man (see Ex. 18).

Jethro, Moses' wife and sons came to see Moses in the wilderness. Jethro heard Moses' testimony of the miraculous things God had done on behalf of His people. Jethro witnessed the justice ministry of Moses for a day. It was after watching Moses meet with person after person from early until late in the day that Jethro rebuked Moses. He reprimanded Moses for settling all the disputes among the people all by himself. His criticism was constructive. He told Moses he was wrong, but he offered clear, concise and wise counsel to make things right. Moses was to equip and release judges who would fulfill the tasks he shouldered alone.

Learn from the Mistakes of Others

Although we should learn from our mistakes, I don't subscribe to the axiom that we must fail to grow. I have certainly made my share of serious errors. I have learned many life lessons from mistakes. But, I would much rather forego the pain and agony of making mistakes. I would much rather learn from the mistakes of others.

The Bible is full of stories of people of faith who entered dynamic relationships with Almighty God. But, it also records the stories of many of the same individuals who messed up royally in their dealings with God and with others. I believe God had the stories of failure recorded so that we could learn from the mistakes of others, enabling us to escape embarrassment, sickness, pain, unhealthy relationships, and even death.

I was nineteen the first time I was certain I heard the voice of God. He got my attention through a sermon preached by our pastor on an otherwise ordinary Sunday morning. I heard His call to ministry as a pastor, but I felt unworthy of such a high calling.

A second sermon a few weeks later, preached by a young college student, convinced me that if I waited until I was worthy to do what God wanted me to do, I would surely wait through eternity. The Lord had my undivided attention.

I already believed the key to real success in life is fulfilling the will of God. His plans for our lives are always good. I wanted to be certain I heard and understood His call correctly. Like Gideon, I asked for a sign from the Lord. My request was not for a specific sign. I only wanted to be certain I had heard His voice before I made a life-changing decision. I wanted to do the will of God with all my heart.

The biblical story of the mistakes of Jonah the prophet helped to guide my decision. God called Jonah to warn the people of Nineveh of impending doom and destruction. Jonah didn't want to warn the enemies of his nation of the coming wrath of His God. Instead, he hoped to witness their utter demise. So, Jonah rebelliously refused to do the will of God. Instead of going to Nineveh he hopped on a boat headed in the opposite direction.

It is at this point in Jonah's story I learned from his mistake. Jonah ended up in the belly of a whale. I would much rather do the will of God than end up the belly of a whale, either literally or figuratively speaking.

Alongside the biblical story of Jonah's rebellion against the will of God, I learned from the mistakes of a man who lived in our community. As I wrestled with clarifying God's call on my life to serve as pastor, I remembered this man's testimony at one of our Sunday evening worship services a few weeks earlier. He told us how he knew God had called him to serve as a pastor, but like Jonah, he had rebelled.

When he shared this testimony, I recall thinking about what I knew about the life this man had lived. He was self-employed as an appliance repairman. His business seemed to be profitable, especially since there was little competition in at least a two-county area. He was an experienced and talented repairman.

His marriage had produced four or five children, some of whom were in my age range. The family occasionally participated in the life of our church.

But, I knew this man spent time in the belly of the whale. He would disappear from his family and the church for weeks at a time. I learned when our church family was called to assist his family that he was a binge alcoholic. He resisted the temptation to drink for a while, then would be overcome. In his testimony, he shared how he believed his refusal to follow God's call on his life had resulted in misery. From my perspective, he was in the belly of a whale.

I earnestly wanted to learn from this man's mistake. I didn't want to end up in the belly of a whale. God is always so good. He was faithful to give me a sign as I requested. It came in the form of a poem written by a person who was also struggling with God's call on his life. His words expressed my reluctance precisely.

God was gracious to speak to me a third time, just as he did young Samuel (see 1 Sam. 3:1-10). This time I heard His whisper, "Feed my sheep." I immediately responded to God's call with a resounding, "Yes, I will go. Here I am, send me!" I began to pursue the training that would enable me to fulfill His high calling. I have never looked back nor regretted stepping into God's plan for my life. It has been an exhilarating adventure with Him!

Listen to Learn God's Plan

God has a plan for every season of our lives—for every moment of every day. Jeremiah 29:11-12 proclaims, "For I know the plans I have for you," declares the Lord, "plans to prosper you and not to harm you, plans to give you hope and a future." If God has astonishing plans for our lives, why would He keep His plans secret from us? He speaks to reveal the calling He has for our lives and His plans for our daily walk with Him. We discover His will only if we are willing to listen to Him.

God spoke to reveal His calling on the lives of leaders we looked at earlier in this chapter: Moses, Nehemiah, David, Gideon, Peter and Jonah. Each of these persons responded to God's call to lead. When they did, their lives and the lives of those the Lord called them to lead were radically transformed. God's plan for the leaders' lives brought freedom for captives, restoration of cities and nations, freedom from oppression, unity, and salvation from destruction and doom for those who followed God and His leaders.

God speaks often directly and very personally to leaders. He called young Samuel and He called Moses, at eighty-years old. He spoke to Samuel in a quiet voice in the night and to a dumbfounded Moses from a burning bush on the mountainside. He often does something supernatural or unusual to get our attention to initiate a conversation with us. God spoke audibly to Samuel as he lay in his bed. He clearly reveals His plan today when we are ready to listen.

The Lord also speaks through others to reveal His call on our lives. Today, He continues to speak to us through apostles, teachers, evangelists, pastors, prophets and other believers to reveal His plans to us. As a leader who is called by God, expect God to speak to you through others.

You will hear the voice of God as you read the Bible if you listen. His followers know His voice. Direction for every season of your life will be abundantly clear as you read the Word of God expecting to hear His clarion call and direction for you.

God has a plan for every moment of every day of our lives. I have discovered the joy of following the direction the old priest Eli gave to young Samuel when he finally realized God was speaking to Samuel. "So Eli told Samuel, 'Go and lie down, and if He calls you, say, 'Speak, Lord, for your servant is listening'" (1 Sam. 3:9). When it is critical for me to learn God's direction or experience His inspiration I go lie down, still my mind, and invite the Holy Spirit to communicate, "Speak, Lord, your servant is listening."

God's call on your life as a leader is good. His plan will prosper you, give you hope and assurance of an exciting future with Him. You and I cannot even imagine the things God has prepared for us. "However, as it is written: "No eye has seen, no ear has heard, no mind has conceived what God has prepared for those who love Him- but God has revealed it to us by His Spirit" (1 Cor. 2:9-10).

Our finite minds cannot imagine the life God has planned for us, but He longs for us to listen to Him as He reveals His will for our lives by His Spirit. His possibilities are infinite! He is Lord of the Impossible!

You lead. Step up to listen!

CHAPTER 3: LEADERS HAVE VISION

Godly leaders seek God's vision for themselves and the persons they lead. God gives leaders a glimpse of the end at the beginning. We see where God wants to take us and we challenge others to go there with us.

In the Kingdom of God, the vision is always greater than us. If the vision is not great, it is not God's vision. If we can accomplish the vision using human ability alone, it is not God's vision. Leaders who diligently pursue an intimate relationship with the Lord and listen attentively to His voice receive His vision.

It is imperative to trust God to enable and equip us to fulfill His vision and to reach His destination for our lives. It is impossible to do it alone. However, we will succeed if we trust and obey the Lord of the Impossible!

God is the Source of vision, and He has a plan for our lives and for those we lead. This is true for families, businesses, schools, states, and nations as well as Christian ministries. It is imperative to listen to Him.

God has a plan for each of our lives. In Jeremiah 29:11-12 He promises, "'For I know the plans I have for you,' declares the Lord, 'plans to prosper you and not to harm you, plans to give you hope and a future.'"

Why would God keep His plans secret from us? He wants us to understand His plan, so we have the life He intends for us. We discover His plan only if we are willing to listen to Him.

His revelation of the plan is the vision. Vision is the experience of vividly seeing and understanding His plan for our future.

Searching for Vision

While a teenager, I began to seek the will of God for my life. I asked Him for direction for my future. In my heart, I knew His plan would give purpose and bring joy and fulfillment. My first experience of clearly and unmistakably hearing His voice came when He called me to serve Him as a pastor when I was nineteen. I had been earnestly praying for His direction for two years. When He spoke, I had no question or doubt He revealed His plan for my life.

Listening to God for His vision for my life and ministry has been very exciting since the day I decided I wanted to submit to His plan. I learned from experience after experience throughout my life, God's plans truly are filled with hope. I have prospered physically, financially, relationally, spiritually and emotionally as I chase after His vision.

Over the years I have grown in both my desire and ability to comprehend and pursue the vision God reveals for my life and ministry.

The most exciting and fulfilling experience of God revealing His vision for me came after twenty years of ministry. Marcia and I had served in four communities before God revealed His vision for us to move to Glasgow, Kentucky.

During my fifth year as shepherd of the Masonville and Utica United Methodist Churches, God surprised us both the same day when He revealed to us His plan for us to go with Him. Although we did not learn where He was sending us until a few months later, we began the next day to pack our possessions in preparation to relocate.

As we earnestly sought the will of God and His plan for ministry, He revealed it through Rick Warren's book, *The Purpose Driven Church* and the Purpose Driven Church Conference I attended. Seeing the big picture vision for ministry so readily was very new to me. I was astonished at how quickly the leadership of the Glasgow United Methodist Church embraced the vision I cast.

The leaders and I began to very intentionally seek God's vision and strategy for our ministry. He was faithful to disclose His will. We understood the need to start new ministries to meet the growing needs of the church and community. The church soon began to grow as new disciples were added weekly. God called more believers to step out in ministry.

As we listened to God, He revealed His strategies to fulfill His vision. We quickly learned God would show every detail of the strategy to accomplish His plan.

One of the best and most exciting examples of God revealing details of strategy to fulfill vision was the children's ministry. The church had a fruitful Sunday school ministry and an amazing children's choir involving children from several community churches. But, we were not doing much to meet the needs of children in our community.

God led us to form a children's ministry team and called a very humble passionate woman to lead. Peggie Marsh began to diligently and earnestly pray for God's direction for meeting the needs of children in our community—often waking in the night to intercede. The children's ministry team joined her to ask God to direct us and to listen for His answer.

Our answer came like a bolt out of the sky one day as I listened to a "Focus on the Family" radio broadcast. James Dobson interviewed leaders from a ministry to children called Kids Hope USA. I knew God was answering prayer. I secured information from that ministry. When the children's ministry team listened to the taped description and testimonies from Kids Hope USA, everyone knew this was God's answer.

We knew we needed a leader for this new ministry who would enable us to pair one mentor with one child in one school for one hour each week. We immediately knew Marianna Irving was God's choice. Marianna had recently retired after thirty-three years as a teacher in one of the local public elementary schools. She was earnestly seeking God's will for her future. She heard and answered God's call.

God revealed His strategy for the Kids Hope USA ministry to Marianna and the Children's Ministry Team. Twelve people volunteered to mentor a child. Twelve more agreed to serve as substitute mentors. An additional twelve people committed to praying for each student, mentor, and substitute. God lead us to mentor at-risk students at the elementary school where Marianna had taught so many years and enjoyed an excellent reputation with the administration and faculty.

Within a few months, over half of the active members of the church were directly involved in some way in the ministry. The first year all twelve of the student's grades improved, some dramatically. The self-esteem and confidence of every child changed. Today this ministry to children is a national model for Kids Hope USA.

Keeping the Focus on God's Vision

We need help to stay focused on His vision. I want faithful intercessors to pray with me as we seek God's direction together. I want people of faith to agree in prayer with me for the power to fulfill God's plan for my life and ministry.

While serving as the Madisonville District Superintendent in the United Methodist Church, I learned the value of prayer partners who intentionally and urgently petition God on behalf of leaders. I had been in Madisonville only a few days when God sent three women from a prayer group to my office to pray with me. They assured me their prayer group had urgently petitioned God to send the right person to lead the district ministry. They believed He had answered their prayers through me.

The Lord began that day to do a new thing in my life. He gave me a new and profound appreciation for intercessors who prayed diligently for me and often with me. Their prayers helped me to discover God's vision for ministry and to stay focused on His plan.

God called many people to intercede on my behalf during that season of my life. One morning I received three phone calls in a brief period from individuals who assured me they were praying urgently for me since the early hours of the day. Each of them wanted to know what was going on in my life and ministry to need such urgent prayer. Each of them insisted God kept bringing me to their mind and was prevailing on them to pray for an extended period. I was not currently experiencing unusual stress nor was I aware of any spiritual attack on my life. I was not sick nor were any of my family members.

I was profoundly grateful for the love these believers poured out on me that morning. I appreciated the compassion they revealed and time they were giving on my behalf. I knew God was teaching me something. A few days later as I reflected on this experience, God gave me a vivid vision. I stood on a battlefield as six soldiers encircled me with their backs to me. Rectangular shields taller than the huge soldiers protected most of their bodies. Flaming arrows arced toward us, but the soldiers caught them with the large shields, protecting both them and me from harm.

I knew the Lord was showing me He had sent prayer warriors for my protection in a raging battle. The shields of prayer and faith lifted by these brave and loyal intercessors protected me. Because of this protection, I was completely unaware the fight was raging around me. This security enabled me to remain focused on God's vision instead of being distracted by the enemy.

Vision is Imperative

Christian leaders must have vision. "Where there is no vision, the people perish" (Prov. 29:18; KJV). God has a plan for our lives, for our life together, and for our world. Vision is simply God's revelation of His plan. It is His desire that we know where He is taking us, so we totally surrender our will to follow His leading.

In Jeremiah 29:11, God promises His plan is always good for us. He reveals His amazing plans for our lives, especially through spiritual leaders by His Spirit. "No eye has seen, no ear has heard, no mind has conceived what God has prepared for those who love Him, but God has revealed it to us by His Spirit" (1 Cor. 2:9-10).

Moses' Vision

Other than Jesus, Moses is the leader in the Bible I respect most and relate to best. God used the call of Moses to enable me to understand His call on my life. The first sermon I preached when I was nineteen years old was from Exodus 3 which describes how God called Moses to lead. The call of Moses enabled me to articulate the call of God on my life. Moses demonstrates some amazing qualities of godly leadership. His example can help us learn to lead effectively.

The people of Israel had suffered in slavery for 400 years. They had no vision. Slavery was all the people knew and experienced for generations. They lost sight of the truth that they were God's people. They, like all people, were created to be free.

The Lord had not forgotten His people in Egypt. He had a plan to bring good, to prosper them and to give the people of Israel hope. God revealed His vision to Moses in the backside of the desert on Mount Horeb. He spoke to Moses from a burning bush.

It was God who initiated the conversation with Moses. He challenged Moses to do what Moses understood from his frail human perspective to be impossible. How could he possibly lead the people of Israel to freedom? Clearly, this was not Moses' idea. Surely Moses had dreamed of seeing Israel free from bondage but certainly didn't think he was the person to lead them.

God's vision for us is always grander than our minds can comprehend. The revelation of His plan for His people was incredible and incomprehensible. The Lord would deliver the people of Israel from Egyptian bondage. He would give them their own land, a good and broad land, flowing with milk and honey. God Almighty would be their God and would be with them always. He would go with them wherever they went to see them through, no matter what.

God initiated this grand vision. He did not speak directly to the entire nation Himself. The Lord only revealed His plan to Moses. He then instructed Moses to articulate this vision first to Aaron, then to the nation's leaders, to the people of Israel, and finally to Pharaoh.

Moses received the vision God revealed and held it in his heart. He faithfully carried God's vision wherever the people traveled throughout their journey to freedom. Moses consistently articulated God's vision for the Israelites as he led them.

Graciously Face Adversity to the Vision

You may articulate the vision God has given you with great wisdom and skill. But, not everyone you encounter or lead will embrace that. Every leader will face adversity from within the ranks. Adversity comes from four types of people. Christian leaders must graciously face adversity from whiners, practical-minded people, people afraid of a challenge and blamers.

1. Whiners

Whiners will stand as roadblocks to the fulfillment of the vision. It seems they are never satisfied or happy with any situation. Everything must go their way, or they complain to leadership.

Whiners expect to be coddled and receive special treatment. When they are not happy, it seems their goal to make certain no one else is happy.

I must admit, I have the hardest time with whiners. I think I probably got that from my father. When we were children, our Dad would not allow my three brothers and me to "whine and carry on." He would listen for a brief time, but then declare in no uncertain terms, "Stop whining or I will give you something to whine about." We always knew for certain he wasn't bluffing.

When I became a father, I soon discovered I had little tolerance for whining. I quickly adopted Dad's line with our three sons, "Stop whining or I will give you something to whine about."

I often wanted to say to whiners in the ministries I led, "Can't you see what God has done? Don't you see what He is doing now? Stop whining and be thankful!" Although I never told people, "Stop whining!" I must admit I often desperately wanted to shout it in their ears.

The people of Israel whined to Moses when they saw the Egyptian army marching toward them at the Red Sea, "Didn't we say to you in Egypt, 'Leave us alone; let us serve the Egyptians?' It would have been better for us to serve the Egyptians than to die in the desert!" (Ex. 14:12). It seems they had no memory of what God did in Egypt with the ten plagues.

Then the people of Israel danced and celebrated God's victory over the Egyptians. But they were murmuring and whining again only three days later when the water they found was bitter. "So the people grumbled against Moses, saying, 'What are we to drink?'" (Ex.15:24). God's patience with His people is evident at Marah when He provided water suitable to consume.

2. Practical people.

Christian leaders must graciously face adversity from rational people who seem only able to envision what humans can do. Somehow, they seldom seem to consider what God can do. They can only see human-sized projects, easily losing sight of the possibility of God-sized miracles. Their faith is often minuscule. It is not unusual that these same persons are successful from the world's perspective. They are among the most respected and resourceful in society.

Practical persons may not express it openly, but their attitude is easily detected, "I got what I have without any help, the hard way, by making realistic, sensible decisions." They fail to see how God gave them opportunities many others did not have available. They fail to realize it was God who gave them wisdom and resources. They frequently fail to give God credit for His part in their successes.

The attitude of the practical, logical person resounds, "If it is too difficult for humans, it won't work." The Israelites with this same attitude said, "Leave us alone; let us serve the Egyptians"(Ex.14:12).

If you and I go with God, we can expect surprises. Human beings often try to press God into our "practical mold." He doesn't ever fit!

Have you ever looked at a biblical map of the Israelite escape route? The Land of Canaan was east of Egypt, but the Israelites marched south! The logical way to Canaan was the "Philistine Way." It was the closest, least difficult way. The other route was further, less comfortable, and most threatening. There was a dead end at the Red Sea. Admittedly, some of the practical Israelites must have objected to traveling the route God chose.

Human logic is radically different from divine wisdom.

I must readily admit, that I more likely fit into this group. I seek the most logical, practical approach. If I, along with other practical people, could only remember the truth, "For my thoughts are not your thoughts, neither are your ways my ways," declares the Lord. As the heavens are higher than the earth, so are my ways higher than your ways and my thoughts than your thoughts" (Is. 55: 8-9).

I want a greater faith in the supernatural surprises of God! I don't want to scold people for small faith. I want to lead and encourage them to greater faith.

3. People Afraid of a Challenge

Christian leaders must graciously face adversity from people who fear challenge. This group is content to stay with the familiar. They resist change in most any form. They are pessimistic and have little faith in what God can do.

The Israelites were afraid. "As Pharaoh approached, the Israelites looked up, and there were the Egyptians, marching after them. They were terrified and cried out to the Lord" (Ex. 14:10).

Remember, these same fearful people witnessed what God did through the plagues in Egypt. Every day they observed the twenty-four-hour supernatural guidance of the Lord in the sky above them on their journey through the wilderness, assuring them God was leading. They heard God's promise with their ears that He would guide, protect, and give them victory over their enemies. They were still afraid.

Are we so different? When challenged, our faith often quickly flies out the window. We are afraid we will not be able to face the challenge. We feel weak.

4. Blamers

Christian leaders must graciously face adversity from blamers. The Israelites blamed, "This is all *your* fault, Moses!"

> They said to Moses, 'Was it because there were no graves in Egypt that *you* brought us to the desert to die? What have *you* done to us by bringing us out of Egypt? Didn't we say to *you* in Egypt, 'Leave us alone; let us serve the Egyptians'? It would have been better for us to serve the Egyptians than to die in the desert!' (Exodus 14: 11-12, emphasis mine)

Sonny Jurgensen was the quarterback for the Washington Redskins football team from 1964 to 1974. One year the football team was in a slump. Fans and media alike were blaming Sonny. Someone asked him, "Is all this flack getting to you?" Jurgensen flashed a big toothless grin, "Naw, not me. I've been in this game long enough to know that every week the quarterback is either in the penthouse or the outhouse." (Story from Chuck Swindoll's *Dropping Your Guard*, pp. 35-36). The penthouse is certainly more fun, but with the blamers, leaders are in the outhouse more often. God's leaders realize this, but stand firm in the Lord.

How do spiritual leaders respond when faced with resistance to the vision? How do you deal graciously with those persons who seem determined to kill the vision?

Grasp the Vison Firmly

Hold firmly to the vision God has given you. Grasp hold of the vision tightly with all you have and do not let go! Keep the main thing the main thing. Don't allow unworthy distractions to sidetrack you. Stay centered and on track.

Realize from the beginning not everyone will embrace the vision. Some who cannot see the destination will refuse to follow your lead. Others see it clearly, but simply do not want to go there.

Be encouraged; there are always some who immediately and wholeheartedly embrace the vision. Others, who process more slowly, will certainly come alongside you somewhere down the road.

Resist the "Elijah Complex."

The prophet Elijah had experienced an incredible victory of faith on Mount Carmel (see 1 Kings 18). Elijah boldly challenged the prophets of the idol gods before a national assembly of the people of Israel.

Baal, the idol god of fire, was unable to set the sacrifice of his prophets aflame. Eight hundred and fifty prophets of the idol god prayed, danced, shouted and slashed themselves for hours, all to no avail. Elijah, in faith, pours barrel after barrel of water on his sacrifice and with a simple two-sentence prayer called down fire from Almighty God. The water, the wood, and the sacrifice were all suddenly consumed. The people of Israel in fear, amazement, and faith prostrated themselves on the ground pledging their allegiance to the God of Elijah.

Within hours Elijah's persistent intercession resulted in God sending a deluge of rain, the first the nation had seen in three and a half years. Then the Spirit of God came on Elijah with such supernatural power that he outran Ahab's chariot on foot. Despite these powerful experiences with God, Elijah was fearful when Jezebel threatened to execute him. He fled for his life.

In 1 Kings 19, we find Elijah cowering in a cave on Mount Horeb after a journey of more than forty days. When the Lord spoke to him in a still small voice Elijah's complex is very evident in his response. "He replied, 'I have been very zealous for the Lord God Almighty. The Israelites have rejected your covenant, broken down your altars, and put your prophets to death with the sword. I am the only one left, and now they are trying to kill me too'" (1 Kings 19:14).

Elijah soon discovered his complaint, "I am all alone, no one else is faithful to you, and I will soon die," and his complex was ill-founded. God reveals the truth, "You are not alone, seven thousand people join you in your faith in Me. I have work left for you to do."

Spiritual leaders will actively and purposefully resist the Elijah Complex. You and I are never alone. God has promised to go with us wherever He sends us. His purposes are sometimes delayed but never thwarted. There is always a remnant of people faithful to the vision of the Kingdom of God who is ready to join you.

Ask God to reveal the believers who are near you and to send others from far away to unite to fulfill His vision. Don't try to change people who cause adversity. Realize only God can change people. After the miracle at the Red Sea, you would think whiners, practical people, those afraid of a challenge, and the blamers would all change. Not so, at least not all of them.

Challenge the People You Lead

At the Red Sea Moses first challenged the people to be still and watch God work on their behalf. "Moses answered the people, 'Do not be afraid. Stand firm and you will see the deliverance the Lord will bring you today. The Egyptians you see today you will never see again. The Lord will fight for you; you need only to be still'" (Ex. 14:13-14).

Obedience to God often involves standing still to watch. The resolution for the people of Israel that day was supernatural. They did not need to strategize or work or fight. God did what only God can do!

Moses issued a second challenge to the people, "Go forward!" You cannot stay where you are and go with God. "Then the Lord said to Moses, 'Why are you crying out to Me? Tell the Israelites to move on'" (Ex. 14:15). Expect God to have a few surprises along the way. The sea parted, and they walked across on dry land. God spared Israel! Unless God challenges His people, they will not learn to trust Him!

Passion for the Vision

Every leader needs passion for the vision God has given. I believe passion is a gift from God. Passion in a spiritual leader is the burning desire to fulfill God's will. God ignited a fire in our bones to partner with Him to accomplish His vision for our lives.

Adversity from whiners, practical-minded people, people afraid of a challenge and blamers can quickly extinguish the fire.

The exceedingly difficult challenges of life often extinguish the flames of our passion. We may be faced with physical illness, physical disabilities due to traumatic experiences, or the death of people we love. God will ignite the flame of passion again, if we only ask Him.

The day-to-day responsibilities and distractions of life slowly quench the flames of passion. I have the most difficulty with daily distractions. Practical duties like meals, dishes, the lawn and landscaping, running errands, and helping care for my parents often smother the flame of passion for accomplishing the things I know and desire to be the highest priorities in my life. The good gets in the way of the noble and great.

God called me to write this book, but far too many times the practical responsibilities of my life took precedent over fulfilling God's will, smothering the flame of passion.

Faith for the Vision

Our purpose as believers is to partner with God to transform our world as we bring the culture of the Kingdom of God to earth. We will only make a difference for the Kingdom if we trust the King. We must rely on His supernatural intervention to effect transformation. It is our faith in Him that enables us to lead change.

"Now faith is being sure of what we hope for and certain of what we do not see" (Heb. 11:1).

Faith is the growing expectation of God's intervention to do impossible things. Faith is trusting God to use us to fulfill His vision. Faith is believing God and acting on what we believe.

All too often we attempt to fulfill the vision God has revealed to us on our own. We frequently only see our meager human resources and fail to envision the vast resources of the Creator of the universe. As a result, our expectations are set far too low. We all too quickly begin to believe God's vision cannot be accomplished because we trust ourselves and our resources. We fail to aim high.

Hope for the Vision

I believe Jesus is the Hope of the world. Leaders without hope cannot lead effectively. As believers, our hope is in Jesus. When every heart honors Him as King, our world will be dramatically different. He is our only hope.

No matter how great our charisma, leadership abilities, or available resources we cannot affect change alone. Our hope is in the One who created the world and knows how to fix the mess we humans have made of it.

My hope increases when I read or hear the testimonies of believers who are experiencing God moving powerfully in their lives. When I read the Bible, my hope intensifies. The testimonies of people Jesus healed, delivered from evil or accepted as friends convinced others to come to Him in faith. I know Jesus has not changed, so He continues to draw people to Himself. He uses ordinary people like you and me to bring hope to His world.

Joy for the Vision

I believe it is God's desire that we experience joy—one of the results (fruits) of His Spirit dwelling in us (see Gal. 5:22-23).

I believe it is the Father's will that every person He created experiences joy in the work they do. You may be leading as a parent or a pastor. You may be the chief executive officer in your company or the chief bottle washer in your home. You may lead in your church or community. It is the Father's will that as a Christian and as a leader you are filled with joy.

I believe the level of joy can be so high that you are willing to do what you do without pay. Centered in the will of God we experience unspeakable joy. When filled with supernatural joy our leadership position will not feel like work. Solomon's journal articulates it perfectly, "So I commend the enjoyment of life, because nothing is better for a man under the sun than to eat and drink and be glad. Then joy will accompany him in his work all the days of the life God has given him under the sun" (Ecc. 8:15).

I have experienced this joy my entire adult life. As a teenager, I began asking God to show me His will for my life. I desperately wanted to center my life in His will. He called me at nineteen years old to my divine destiny as a pastor.

When God used my parents, my pastor and several long-term friends to confirm the vision to serve as pastor, I had a sense of great relief. I knew what God wanted me to do with my life! Such indescribable joy filled my life that my family and closest friends told me later, "Your feet didn't seem to touch the ground for months after you experienced God's call."

When I asked God to show me how He wanted to equip me for ministry as a pastor, He quickly revealed I was to transfer from the state university to a Christian college. Although I had never considered graduate studies, His direction to pursue a Master of Divinity degree came on the heels of the call. I experienced joy in my journey to receive an education that prepared me well for leading as a pastor.

At the end of my first year of seminary, God led me to serve in the United Methodist Church. I knew from the bottom of my heart that God led me to the United Methodist Church in Kentucky. Wherever He led me as youth pastor, chaplain, associate pastor, senior pastor and district superintendent I experienced joy.

I frequently affirmed my love for ministry. "I love my job. I would do it without pay if I didn't need money to live." The foundation of the joy I have experienced throughout my life has been discovering God's vision for my life and trying to the best of my ability to gladly be where He wanted me to be and to do what He wanted me to do.

As a pastor, I talked to many people about their lives and the absence of joy they experienced. Although I did not do a scientific survey or keep careful records, I believe seventy-five percent or more of the people I knew and talked to did not like the work they were doing. Most of them felt they were making little difference in their company or the Kingdom of God. As a result, joy was missing from their lives.

When we focus intently on God's priorities for our lives, joy is overwhelming. Jesus spoke of discovering God's priority of the Kingdom of God in this simple parable: "The kingdom of heaven is like treasure hidden in a field. When a man found it, he hid it again, and then in his joy went and sold all he had and bought that field" (Matt. 13:44). When we seek the will of God and embrace it with all we are, the Spirit fills us with great joy.

Jesus promised, "If you obey My commands, you will remain in My love, just as I have obeyed My Father's commands and remain in His love. I have told you this so that My joy may be in you and that your joy may be complete. My command is this: Love each other as I have loved you" (Jn. 15:10-12).

We experience complete joy when we obediently love each other. It is the second greatest priority for Him.

Jesus discovered complete joy as He fulfilled His divine destiny. "Let us fix our eyes on Jesus, the author and perfecter of our faith, who for the joy set before Him endured the cross, scorning its shame, and sat down at the right hand of the throne of God" (Heb. 12:2). Jesus progressively understood His destiny meant extreme pain, physical and emotional suffering, being deserted by followers and friends, and experiencing His Father turning His face from Him. Jesus pursued the destiny to which God had called Him with unspeakable joy.

No Distractions

Leaders must say "No" to all distractions preventing them from pursuing God's vision. Distractions cause us to take our eyes off God's priorities. Distractions will come. Distractions will often be in your space and in your face. Some distractions are small, while others loom large. Sometimes the distractions are very brief and temporary. Sometimes they are significant and last for long periods of time. Many, if not most of the distractions for the Christian leader will be good, worthy things.

If we fulfill our divine destinies to produce fruit in the Kingdom of God it is vital that we keep our eyes focused on God's vision. When we look away from the vision, especially for long periods of time we lose our grip and our passion to fulfill the vision. Keep the main thing the main thing.

The main thing is God's vision for our lives and ministry.

It is important to live life very intentionally. Whatever I am doing, I am a "man on a mission." That is true for the ordinary chores of life like mowing the lawn, helping do laundry or shopping at Walmart.

I often describe myself as having a "one-track-mind." I don't multi-task well at all and I am so focused on my mission I sometimes totally miss something more important. I must confess I can be like the priest or the Levite in Jesus' Parable of the Good Samaritan, not because I lack compassion, but I am so laser focused on accomplishing the practical day-to-day mission that I don't even see the man on the side of the road. Sometimes a distraction is an opportunity to fulfill God's Kingdom vision.

Helping to care for our aging parents is the primary reason my wife and I earnestly believe God sent us back to North Carolina. Two months after hearing God's call to write this book my eighty-four-year old mother was diagnosed with pancreatic cancer. Her health began to seriously deteriorate very quickly. I helped to get her to frequent radiation treatments. I helped her and my Dad with some of their daily needs. I spent hours with her in the hospital or at home when she needed twenty-four-hour care.

My priorities changed so I did not write for three months. I have no regrets or guilt. The vision the Lord gave me to write the book did not fade, but it slipped down my list of priorities during the time of Mom's illness and death. Sometimes we face situations in our lives requiring us to take our eyes off the vision. We must return quickly to God's vision for our lives and ministry.

Keep your mind and your heart laser-focused on God's vision for your life and ministry. Jesus challenges us, "But seek first His kingdom and His righteousness, and all these things will be given to you as well" (Matt. 6:33). With these words, He promises if we chase after His vision He will take care of all the distractions and all the practical aspects of life: where we will live, what we will eat and the clothes we will wear. Adamantly refuse to allow distractions to side-track you from fulfilling God's vision for your life and ministry.

You lead. Step up to discover and fulfill God's vision!

CHAPTER 4: LEADERS AIM HIGH

Leaders set their hearts on perfection. God created us in His image. The Lord is perfect. As a leader, my heart's desire is to be perfect as He is perfect (see Matt. 5:48). There is a fine line between the desire to be perfect and perfectionism. I have fallen into the latter much of my life. Perfectionism is trying to earn approval by performance. Every attempt to gain approval leads to the fear of failure.

We often feel we don't measure up when we expect to please either ourselves or others entirely. Failing to be perfect in our own eyes or the eyes of others quickly leads to worry, depression, anxiety, and a host of other issues that prevent us from reaching our potential as leaders.

We are challenged as Christian believers to aim high. We will sometimes miss the mark. Our arrows fall short of the target. We will make mistakes and sin. Although we are imperfect human beings who never consistently hit the mark of perfection, this should never stop us from aiming high.

Today God has called spiritual leaders to a higher standard in their personal lives. It is not a new standard. It is the benchmark found in God's word. He has drawn a line. To cross the line is to disobey. In our personal lives and the life of a church, community, city, region or nation there comes the point when God draws a line. What He once tolerated, He no longer tolerates. God's benchmark for spiritual leaders is that we be above reproach.

> Here is a trustworthy saying: If anyone sets his heart on being an overseer, he desires a noble task. *Now the overseer must be above reproach,* the husband of but one wife, temperate, self-controlled, respectable, hospitable, able to teach, not given to drunkenness, not violent but gentle, not quarrelsome, not a lover of money. He must manage his own family well and see that his children obey him with proper respect. (If anyone does not know how to manage his own family,

how can he take care of God's church?) He must not be a recent convert, or he may become conceited and fall under the same judgment as the devil. He must also have a good reputation with outsiders, so that he will not fall into disgrace and into the devil's trap. (1 Timothy 3:1-7; emphasis mine)

In the ancient Greek culture, an overseer was the presiding official in a civic or religious organization. Paul was writing to Timothy, his son in the faith, concerning persons who served as overseers of local congregations. The duties of the overseer or elder were to teach and preach, to direct the affairs of the church, to shepherd God's flock (see Acts 20:28), and to guard the faith against error (see Acts 20:29-31). Leading as an overseer is "a noble task" in the eyes of God.

In 1 Timothy 3:1-7 Paul enables us to get a clear picture of the target at which we aim as spiritual leaders. As we read his words, the target comes into focus as though we were looking through a rifle scope. He lines the crosshairs of the scope on the bullseye. Aim at the center to reach the goal of healthy, spiritual relationships with family members, the people on your team and the people you serve.

"Temperate" describes your moderate, self-controlled, reasonable and calm approach to people and problems. If we ignore either people or problems, we miss the target. When we allow either to rattle us, we fall short of the intended mark.

In 1 Timothy 3, Paul declares that an identifying mark of a leader who aims high is faithful, monogamous, in a heterosexual marital relationship. The Biblical benchmark is the marriage of one man to one woman. Anything short of that mark is rebellion and sin against Almighty God, our Creator.

Leaders who aim high are not given to drunkenness, not violent and not quarrelsome. Addictions to drugs or alcohol have no place in the life of any leader. Impaired thinking and judgement, conflict and violence are the consequences of these addictions.

Spiritual leaders show hospitality especially in their sphere of influence. Genuine hospitality seems well on its way to becoming a lost and dying art in today's world.

Marcia and I experienced delightful hospitality at a small-town movie theater. We drove up to the front of the theater on a sunny afternoon to look at the posters to learn what movies were playing. A professionally dressed attendant seated comfortably in the ticket booth quickly stepped out onto the sidewalk to greet us. "It is a good day to see a movie. Where are you folks from?" After we had responded he recommended the matinee viewing of "The Notebook."

When we returned later in the afternoon to purchase tickets for the movie he again stepped out of the booth to introduce himself and to escort us into the dark theater with his flashlight. We had not experienced that kind of genuine, warm hospitality anywhere, even in the many churches we were visiting at the time.

Spiritual Leadership Qualifications

We find the requirements for admission into spiritual leadership in God's Word in several passages. In Acts 6:1-7, Luke identifies three characteristics: the leader is to be full of faith, full of wisdom and full of the Spirit.

> In those days when the number of disciples was increasing, the Hellenistic Jews among them complained against the Hebraic Jews because their widows were being overlooked in the daily distribution of food. So the Twelve gathered all the disciples together and said, "It would not be right for us to neglect the ministry of the word of God in order to wait on tables. Brothers, choose seven men from among you who are known to be full of the Spirit and wisdom. We will turn this responsibility over to them and will give our attention to prayer and the ministry of the word." This proposal pleased the whole group. They chose Stephen, a man full of faith and of the Holy Spirit; also Philip, Procorus, Nicanor, Timon, Parmenas, and Nicolas from Antioch, a convert to Judaism. They presented these men to the apostles, who prayed and laid their hands on them. So the word of God spread. The number of disciples in Jerusalem increased rapidly, and a large number of priests became obedient to the faith.

In the early days of the Jerusalem church born on the Day of Pentecost, the need arose for additional leadership. The twelve disciples whom Jesus had commissioned to lead discovered they were unable to meet the demands of both teaching and coordinating service to persons in need. They needed assistance to fulfill the practical, physical needs of widows. Notice that even those who were to serve tables needed the same spiritual qualities as the twelve.

Today, as we select leaders to serve alongside us in ministry or the marketplace, we look for the same spiritual qualifications. We seek believers who are full of faith, wisdom, and the Holy Spirit.

Aim high for persons full of faith. These believers trust God implicitly. They believe God is in control and nothing is impossible with Him. They listen to God to learn what He is doing and join Him. Their goals and dreams are beyond human achievement, requiring divine action and intervention. Their vision cannot be accomplished unless and until God moves.

When the storms of life rage around believers who are full of faith, they don't give up, and they don't give in. They declare with conviction, "But God..."

Today, we seek believers who are full of wisdom. "The fear of the Lord is the beginning of knowledge, but fools despise wisdom and discipline" (Prov. 1:7). The persons we want to serve with us reverently honor the Lord, trusting Him to guide their daily lives. These believers carefully consider the consequences their decisions and actions will have on their own lives and the lives of others. (Chapter 7, "Leaders Seek Wisdom" is devoted entirely to this subject).

Today, we seek believers who are full of the Holy Spirit. Spotting believers full of the Holy Spirit is easy. These persons seem to always be in the right place at the right time to partner with God to bring transformation to the lives of others. They live thankful lives and are always ready to praise God and give Him the glory. Like Jesus, their lives reflect the authority and power given to them as children of the King of kings. Love, joy, peace, patience, kindness, goodness, faithfulness, gentleness and self-control flow unceasingly from our lives when we are full of the Holy Spirit (see Gal. 5:22-23).

When you partner with other leaders in your family, ministry, work or school who are full of faith, wisdom and the Holy Spirit you aim high. Refuse to accept status quo and join God to experience the extraordinary and supernatural.

A Word of Caution

Don't get so far ahead of those you lead that they cannot see you. Our heart's desire is to lead people on a journey to reach their divine destiny. We do this by walking alongside them, sharing the journey. We challenge them to seek God's plan for their lives, to aim higher, to keep going when the going is tough, to trust God, and to never give up.

Spiritual leaders experience God and listen to His voice. The Lord reveals where He wants to take us and those we lead. There is nothing more important to me than discovering the will of God for my life. Previous adventures with Him were packed with excitement and joy. So, when He reveals a new venture, I am usually ready to rise immediately to follow Him.

Past experiences have proven that not everyone I lead catches God's vision quickly. Some are willing to aim high with God immediately. Others need time to process what it will mean for their lives. Another group wants to aim high with God but are not willing to make the necessary sacrifices to get there. Some just want to go their own way.

In June 2001, God sent me to lead pastors. As a leader of leaders, God soon revealed the need to share this word of caution with them.

Throughout the five years I served as district superintendent in the United Methodist Church, pastors often had powerful, life-changing experiences with God. Their trust and faith in Him grew exponentially.

Out of love and a burning desire for the members of their congregations to experience God and to grow in their faith the pastors led with passion. Sometimes the revelation of God and their experiences with God caused them to run ahead of the people they led.

There is always a great need to challenge the people we lead by going where others are afraid to go. But, as we lead, we can get so far ahead that our followers can no longer see us. They cannot follow us if they cannot see us. Don't get so far ahead of the people you lead that they cannot see you.

His Ways Are High

Spiritual leaders aim high because God's vision and mission are always higher than ours. His possibilities are always greater than our potential.

> For My thoughts are not your thoughts,
>   neither are your ways My ways," declares the Lord.
> As the heavens are higher than the earth,
>   so are My ways higher than your ways
> and My thoughts than your thoughts. (Isaiah 55:8-9)

We pursue His high calling in our lives. When we experience God's call to spiritual leadership we cannot possibly imagine how He will work supernaturally in our lives to fulfill the divine destiny He envisions. His resources and supernatural abilities are endless.

The Lord delights in us when we give ourselves unreservedly to partner with Him to fulfill His purposes. He gave us the greatest gift possible when He came to live with us in Jesus. The Spirit of Christ dwells richly in every believer, giving us power to be so much more than we would be. He has given His best. He requires our best. He seeks those who will aim high to live holy lives fully surrendered to His will and purpose.

Ours is a journey pursuing excellence in our lives and ministry. We aim for the high calling and high ways of our Lord. We praise the Lord for His unfailing forgiveness when we fall short of His mark.

You lead. Step up to aim high!

CHAPTER 5: LEADERS SERVE

Jesus is the greatest leader the world has ever known. At the core of His extraordinary leadership is His heart to serve.

> Jesus called them together and said, 'You know that the rulers of the Gentiles lord it over them, and their high officials exercise authority over them. Not so with you. Instead, whoever wants to become great among you must be your servant, and whoever wants to be first must be your slave— just as the Son of Man did not come to be served, but to serve, and to give His life as a ransom for many.' (Matthew 20:25-28)

It is Jesus' very nature and character to serve. He was a great leader because He knew His purpose and destiny on earth was to serve. He took servanthood to its highest level when He willingly laid his life down for the sake of others.

Instead of jockeying for the most elevated position, Jesus invited His students to be willing to serve. If you desire to be a great spiritual leader, you must be prepared to serve. You must embrace your identity as a servant.

Earn Respect

Persons in leadership positions over us convey authority to us. However, respect is earned, not conveyed. As leaders, we either demand and command respect, or we win it. In Western culture, our dominant practice is to command respect.

When a person has worked hard to come into a position of authority their attitude often is "I earned this position, and you will do what I say." Persons subject to their leadership are forced to follow, or else. Respect is often coerced using subtle, covert, or very overt tactics.

Employees experience the threat of termination. Spouses and children are physically, verbally, and emotionally abused. Athletes face intimidation by coaches on sports teams. Soldiers are often intimidated from the first day of military training to obey those in command.

Real leaders earn respect. Jesus earned the respect of friends and enemies alike. The religious leaders respected Jesus because He taught the truth without reservation. Political leaders recognized His wisdom when they confronted Him. Everywhere He traveled people appreciated the love He tangibly demonstrated for them.

Jesus earned respect because His love was real. He related to ordinary folks whom He encountered day by day. He understood the struggle and shame of the woman at the well (see Jn. 4:4-30). He gladly ate in the homes of the outcasts of society like Zacchaeus (see Luke 19:1-10). He offered His Father's healing power to the sick who came to Him. He willingly extended His forgiveness to the sexually immoral (see Jn. 8:2-11) and hardened criminals (see Lk. 23:39-43).

Lead Gently

He tends His flock like a shepherd:
   He gathers the lambs in His arms
and carries them close to His heart;
   He gently leads those that
have young. (Is. 40:11)

This verse describes both God the Father and Jesus the Son. Both are accurately described as Shepherd. Jesus identified Himself as the Good Shepherd (see Jn. 10:11,14). He leads gently, with compassion. He radically loves those who follow Him. There is no intimidation or harshness in His leadership. He does not force anyone to follow Him. His desire to take us with Him is so great He willingly carries us. He loves everyone who is compromised in any way.

Jesus' deepest desire is to enjoy a personal relationship with those who go with Him. "I am the Good Shepherd; I know My sheep and My sheep know Me— just as the Father knows Me and I know the Father—and I lay down My life for the sheep." (Jn. 10:14-15)

As spiritual leaders, like Jesus, we desire to know those in our care personally. We are vulnerable, allowing those we shepherd to get to know us. Jesus willingly laid down His life to win the hearts of a world full of wanderers like us. He leads gently out of a heart so full of love there is no place for anything else.

Lead Humbly

"Humble yourselves before the Lord, and He will lift you up" (Jas. 4:10).

Humility is a hallmark of a great servant leader from God's perspective. "The greatest among you will be your servant. For whoever exalts himself will be humbled, and whoever humbles himself will be exalted" (Matt. 23:11-12). God promises to promote the humble to the highest positions.

If we refuse to humble ourselves, there are times the Lord moves to humble us. "Remember how the Lord your God led you all the way in the wilderness these forty years, to humble and test you in order to know what was in your heart, whether or not you would keep His commands" (Deut. 8:2).

God's process of humbling and testing the children of Israel was long, yet filled with grace. Forty years is a long time to be disciplined by the Lord. But every day He guided them carefully, fed them manna, and protected their clothes and shoes from wear. Such powerful evidence of God's amazing grace!

Jesus is the supreme example of servant leadership. No leader throughout history compares to Him. He is the greatest leader the world has ever known. The nature of this great leader is described in Philippians 2:5-11:

> Your attitude should be the same as that Christ Jesus: Who, being in very nature God, did not consider equality with God something to be grasped, but made Himself nothing, taking the very nature of a servant, being made in human likeness. And being found in appearance as a man, He humbled Himself and became obedient to death—even death on a cross! Therefore God exalted Him to the highest place and gave Him the name that is above every name, that at the name of Jesus every knee should bow, in heaven and on earth and under the earth, and every tongue confess that Jesus Christ is Lord, to the glory of God the Father.

The greatest leader the world has ever known lived His entire life as a servant. He came to our world to serve. He gave up His rightful place on a royal throne in heaven next to God to come to earth to serve. He was born in a stable, gladly associated with the lowest of society, washed dirty feet, suffered humiliation as a criminal and died on a cruel cross.

Marcia's Example

What does being a servant leader look like in today's world? I see a beautiful picture of servant leadership when I look at my wife, Marcia. She continually serves at home, with our extended families, in her work and the life of the church. I have watched her race to serve before most of us even have the thought that someone has a need.

When her side of the family has one of its frequent gatherings for a holiday or someone's birthday, she serves. There are always plenty of opportunities to serve when the Higgins clan gathers—potentially 25-50 persons from four generations.

Before the family gatherings, Marcia has helped to plan, shopped for groceries, cooked several dishes, helped set up tables and chairs, helped to carry the food and arrange it on the tables.

When the meal begins, instead of filling her plate, she serves the drinks and is one of the last persons in the serving line. Marcia seems always to be aware and ready to help if someone needs a drink refill, a clean fork, or a dessert. It always takes her longer to eat her meal because she is frequently on her feet serving. She seldom takes the time to finish her meal.

When the meal is over, Marcia is usually the first person to get started with the clean-up detail. She most often takes the lead to remove food from the table and wash the dishes. Her service is never complete until after most everyone leaves when she sweeps the floors.

It makes me tired sitting here at the computer just thinking about all the work she does to serve the family. All this comes naturally for her. She seldom asks others to help, but appreciates it when they do. She is the epitome of Jesus' friend Martha, minus the complaining. Marcia serves with a friendly smile on her face and with joy in her heart. She views serving as a calling and gladly accepts it as a part of her destiny.

Marcia has ministered to the physical and medical needs of others as a registered nurse for nearly thirty years. She is most comfortable and happiest when she is doing bedside nursing, caring for the patients directly. She is both professional and friendly. The peace and joy she carries as she serves are apparent to staff, patients and their families alike.

It was her compassionate and joyful servant leadership that opened the door for her to step into a management position in a hospice inpatient unit. She worked there first as a nurse, caring for the patients for about two and a half years. She was confronted daily with dealing emotionally and spiritually with the death of patients.

Following the critical illness and death of her father and my mother during that same time frame, she needed a change. She moved to another health care provider to work as a home health nurse.

Several months after leaving the hospice unit she went back to return her name badge. Upon entering the unit, she was greeted by several members of the staff in tears. They were overjoyed to see her again and expressed their grief in missing her. Several of her peers and previous supervisors then began to beg her to apply for the nurse manager's position.

As a servant leader, she fostered close and healthy relationships with all the persons with whom she worked. Marcia applied for the job and soon the administrative leaders were expressing their appreciation for her and looking forward to working with her.

Marica's servant heart is apparent to everyone who knows her. I believe it was her servant's heart that God used to open the door for her current ministry as the nurse manager of the hospice inpatient unit. She continues to pour out her heart and life in service to God, staff, patients and their families.

Serving Requires Sacrifice

"Jesus announced, "For whoever wants to save his life will lose it, but whoever loses his life for Me and for the gospel will save it" (Mark 8:35).

Serving requires sacrifice. Effective spiritual leaders willingly give their time, talent, and treasure to serve others.

I lead a ministry of healing through our local church. Every Thursday evening our team sacrifices a part of their lives to partner with God to transform the lives of those who often have no life. We give our lives so others can have a life. We intercede on behalf of the sick, depressed, oppressed, brokenhearted, grieving, confused and lonely who need to experience the life-giving power of Father God. As we agree in prayer with them, we watch God restore and transform lives.

We give a part of our lives so that others can have life. We give out of hearts filled with love and compassion. Our sacrifice is minuscule compared to the sacrifice Jesus made on behalf of us all.

Jesus made the ultimate sacrifice of His life so that we could have life. Spiritual leaders follow the example of our Lord as we give our lives for the sake of others. As we give, the Lord fills us with life. We are encouraged, satisfied, and inspired to give more as we sacrifice for the sake of others.

The Lord always fulfills His promise to us as we give to others, "Give, and it will be given to you. A good measure, pressed down, shaken together and running over, will be poured into your lap. For with the measure you use, it will be measured to you" (Lk. 6:38).

In ministry settings, we often conclude we have received much more than we gave, no matter how significant our sacrifice.

The sacrifice required of leaders is personally unique. What is a great sacrifice for one leader may not feel like sacrifice to another leader.

If we don't have healthy and close relationships with family, leaving them for extended periods may not feel like much of a sacrifice. But, for those of us who enjoy being with family and desire to be close geographically to enable us to spend quality time with them, to leave them is great sacrifice. Frequently, to be a servant leader in the kingdom of God requires leaving our families. Jesus promises the reward for sacrificially following Him will be worth it.

Finish Well

Faithfully serve to the end of your life. Where you start is not nearly as important as where you end up. Jesus told the parable of the two sons in Matthew 21:28-30. The father in this parable has the vision of a great harvest from his vineyard. The assistance of his sons is required to fulfill his vision. The first son did not start well. He had no desire to be a part of his father's vision. He rebelliously disobeyed his father, refusing to work in the vineyard. But, he later changed his mind. He repented, turning from disobedience to obedience. The first son did not start well but ended up in faithful obedience.

Spiritual leaders long to finish well. We realize throughout our journey we sometimes failed to start immediately and we fell many times along the way. But, our heart's desire is to do the will of our Father until our journey ends in death. We aspire to serve the Lord and others all our days.

Servant Leadership

Spiritual leaders often find themselves needing to do what others are unable or unwilling to do. We serve in ways we didn't expect when God first revealed His vison to us. There have been times as a pastor when circumstances dictated I did secretarial work, mowed the church lawn or cleaned bathrooms. These responsibilities were not in my job descriptions, but I needed to be willing to fulfill them to demonstrate servant leadership. It is my desire to be willing to do anything I request of staff or volunteers.

Spiritual leaders model genuine servanthood, yet we will not accomplish the will of God for our lives if we fail to equip and release others who are called. If we keep our focus on God's vision for our lives and the lives of those we lead we will need to delegate the responsibilities for the mission others are called and equipped to accomplish. When we equip and release others we are truly serving the Lord and those we lead.

We model servant leadership when we lead humbly and gently. We earn the respect of those we lead when we are willing to do anything and everything we request of others. Jesus exhibited servant leadership at its best and most practical level when He washed feet. Are you and I willing to serve by washing feet today?

You lead. Step up to serve!

CHAPTER 6: LEADERS DESIRE PURITY

"Create in me a pure heart, O God, and renew a steadfast spirit within me" (Ps. 51:10). A spiritual leader's cry is for a heart that is clean and pure. We know we cannot achieve or earn this in our own power. A pure heart is a gift from God.

We sincerely desire His forgiveness when our hearts are stained dark by sin. Our hearts are dark and dirty until they are washed clean by the blood of Jesus. We need His power to overcome temptations.

A pure heart begins with a pure thought life. From one perspective, we have little control over the thoughts that come to our minds. But, we can control what we feed our minds, which affects how we think.

"Garbage in, garbage out." If we fill our minds with violent television, movies, and media, we are more likely to think violent thoughts. If we fill our minds with pornography, we are more likely to think sexually perverted thoughts.

We can control more of our thought life, according to the focus of our priorities each day. When we worship, pray, and read the Word of God daily, our thoughts are more likely to be pure.

"Finally, brothers, whatever is true, whatever is noble, whatever is right, whatever is pure, whatever is lovely, whatever is admirable—if anything is excellent or praiseworthy—think about such things" (Phil. 4:8).

When we direct our thoughts to these things, there is often little time left to have impure thoughts.

"Who may ascend the hill of the LORD? Who may stand in His holy place? He who has clean hands and a pure heart, who does not trust in an idol or swear by what is false" (Ps. 24:3-4).

Our hands are dirty when we participate in evil. Innocent blood covers our hands. Our hands easily become dirty when we are idle. As spiritual leaders, we do not use our hands to do evil or violent acts. A spiritual leader's ultimate desire is to be able to lift holy hands to the Lord in praise and prayer. "I want men everywhere to lift up holy hands in prayer, without anger or disputing" (1 Tim. 2:8).

Character Must Accompany Authority

Integrity is a vital character trait of a leader. A leader's integrity is as important for the world's systems as it is in the Kingdom of God. Leaders who lack integrity will eventually fall. A leader who lacks integrity may muscle and manipulate those under his or her authority in such a manner to delay the fall, but a lack of integrity will soon catch up. ... "and you may be sure that your sin will find you out" (Num. 32:23).

Authority is conveyed to a leader by an institution, a company, a government, a church, or other entity. Those selected for positions of leadership often have training, experience, charisma, and the ability to communicate effectively. But, without the willingness to use the authority with integrity, a fall is inevitable. History is replete with examples: Judas, Adolf Hitler, Benito Mussolini, Joseph Stalin, Fidel Castro, and Richard Nixon.

"Everyone must submit himself to the governing authorities, for there is no authority except that which God has established. The authorities that exist have been established by God" (Rom. 13:1). God sets us all in positions of leadership—as parents, teachers, chief executive officers, pastors, governors, or presidents. He equips us all to lead in a manner that brings His kingdom on earth as it is in heaven in our homes, schools, businesses, churches, and nations.

The Lord gives the spiritual gift of leadership to persons who will receive it and use it to honor Him. He offers the gift of leadership and calls us to lead diligently (see Rom. 12:8).

Keep Your Promises

In the Parable of the Two Sons in Matthew 21:28-31 Jesus emphasized the necessity to precisely fulfill what you vow before God. The father requested his son to work in the vineyard. The son refused. He went to his other son and asked him to work in the vineyard. He promised to go, but he did not go. The first son changed his mind and went to work in the vineyard. Even those with little integrity to whom Jesus told the parable knew the son who at first refused to go but changed his mind did the will of his father.

Ecclesiastes 5:1-5 wisely guides us to think long and hard prior to making promises to God. It is better to not make a promise than to break a promise we make to God.

Guard your steps when you go to the house of God.
Go near to listen rather than to offer the sacrifice of fools,

who do not know that they do wrong.
Do not be quick with your mouth,
 do not be hasty in your heart
  to utter anything before God.
God is in heaven
 and you are on earth,
  so let your words be few.
As a dream comes when there are many cares,
 so the speech of a fool when there are many words.
When you make a vow to God,
 do not delay fulfilling it.
He has no pleasure in fools; fulfill your vow.
 It is better not to make a vow
  than to make one and not fulfill it.

Keep the promises you make to those you lead. Immediately following the inauguration of new presidential leaders our country begins to focus on one thing: will the new president keep the promises made during the campaign? When a new CEO takes office, the staff wonders from the beginning if she will be faithful to keep the promises she makes. When a teacher steps into a classroom for the first time his students expect him to keep the promises made. Children's relationships with their parents are dependent in large part on whether their mother and father are faithful to keep their promises. Make no spontaneous, rash promises you cannot fulfill.

Guard Your Heart

"Above all else, guard your heart, for it is the wellspring of life" (Prov. 4:23). If we desire purity in our lives, we must set a guard over our hearts.

Our hearts turn quickly and easily to sin and evil. We are tempted to leave the way of the Lord, veering off to pursue our own desires. The strongest temptations in your life may differ from mine, but we all are tempted to turn from the straight and narrow path that leads to life. Guard your heart.

Protect your heart from the temptation to turn from the love of God to the love of money. "People who want to get rich fall into temptation and a trap and into many foolish and harmful desires that plunge men into ruin and destruction. For the love of money is a root of all kinds of evil. Some people, eager for money, have wandered from the faith and pierced themselves with many griefs" (1Tim. 6:9-10).

Contentment will help to protect your heart from the love of money. Contentment is a learned response to the circumstances of life. We can emulate Paul who declared he had learned to be content no matter if his resources were abundant or he was in dire need. Paul declared,

I am not saying this because I am in need, for I have learned to be content whatever the circumstances. I know what it is to be in need, and I know what it is to have plenty. I have learned the secret of being content in any and every situation, whether well fed or hungry, whether living in plenty or in want. I can do everything through Him who gives me strength. (Philippians 4:11-13)

Trust will help protect your heart from the love of money. Trust God to give you the strength to find contentment. You can fully trust Him to supply all your needs. After all, He owns the cattle on a thousand hills, and the hills too!

Recognition

Protect your heart from the desire for prestige and recognition. Fame is usually short lived, especially in our modern-day society. Celebrity status is fleeting. Prestige is geographically relative. God helped me realize this many years ago when a local civic club recognized my ministry in the church and community when they gave me their "Outstanding Young Religious Leader Award" for the year. I have never forgotten how I felt a few days later walking down the street of our town.

God revealed the truth that the recognition I had received meant nothing to the average person I met that day on the street. Someone from my church, who was a member of the civic club, had nominated me to receive the award. Many members who did not know me had voted to give the award to me that year. A small number of people from my church read about the award in the newspaper. But, few other people would know I had received the award. Most people I met on the street that day could have cared less.

Prestige and fame are geographically relative. As I continued to walk down the street, I thought of people who should be well-known in my state, like the governor. I knew the name of the governor of Kentucky, where we lived. I wasn't confident I would recognize him if we passed on the street. I realized I knew almost nothing about him. I then recognized I didn't even know the names of the governors of two of the adjoining states: Tennessee and Indiana. Prestige truly is very relative and short-lived.

Sexual Promiscuity

Guard your heart against sexual promiscuity, adultery, and sexual immorality. Sexual sins have a disastrous impact on everyone directly involved and on many innocent spouses, children, family members, friends, neighbors, and society itself.

Don't flirt with persons of the opposite sex. You are playing with fire that first burns you and then ignites a raging forest fire. Sexually suggestive comments and physical touches are always inappropriate for anyone, especially leaders.

Men, don't take that second look. Instead of looking lustfully at a woman's body, look at her face and eyes. Intentionally look the other direction instead of gazing long at her body. Turn your eyes in the opposite direction.

Heed Paul's advice, *"Flee from sexual immorality.* All other sins a man commits are outside his body, but he who sins sexually, sins against his own body" (1 Cor. 6:18, emphasis mine). We overcome any temptation by quickly removing ourselves from it. Run swiftly from sexual temptations.

Joseph is an excellent model for us to follow to avoid sexual temptation. When Potiphar's wife noticed Joseph's handsome, well-built body she began to seduce him sexually. Joseph quickly and without apology rejected this temptation, proclaiming his allegiance to Potiphar, his appreciation for his position and his commitment to being faithful to God.

Undeterred, Potiphar's wife continued to try to seduce Joseph. Today, she would be found guilty of sexual harassment in the workplace. Joseph's reasoned response to overcome any temptation was to do all he could to avoid her. "And though she spoke to Joseph day after day, he refused to go to bed with her or even be with her" (Gen. 39:10). But, since Potiphar's home was Joseph's workplace it became impossible to escape her.

One day when they were alone in the house, Potiphar's wife once again attempted to seduce him. Joseph's response was exemplary—he fled from the house. Although the rest of the story finds the innocent Joseph imprisoned, he made the right decision. It is always the right choice for us as leaders to flee sexual temptation and seduction.

Flee temptation—run as fast as you possibly can run. Escape swiftly, because your life does depend on it. Escape the way Joseph fled from Potiphar's wife, leaving his robe behind. "Flee the evil desires of youth, and pursue righteousness, faith, love and peace, along with those who call on the Lord out of a pure heart" (2 Tim. 2:22).

Most men face the strong temptation to view pornography. Guard your heart. Your eyes become the gateway for the heart to enter a dark and perverted world. If the temptation is strong in your life, move now to set guards. Ask your spouse or another male (or female if tempted as a woman) to hold you accountable to refuse to view pornography.

Enlist this person to set password protected boundaries on all your media devices. Don't enter any business where you will endure temptation. Turn off and delete movies and media whenever lured into viewing soft or hardcore pornography.

"And the peace of God, which transcends all understanding, will guard your hearts and your minds in Christ Jesus" (Phil. 4:7). Seek the amazing gift of God's peace to guard your heart. Peace is not something we earn or deserve. It is simply a gift offered freely to us through the atoning sacrifice of Jesus.

Be Vulnerable

Although it may be our heart's desire to be pure, we all sin. The hands and heart of every person get dirty. When David cries out to God in Psalm 51 for a pure heart, he knows he cannot in his own power wash his own heart clean. No amount of soap and water will wash away the guilt and shame (see Jer. 2:22). He must repent.

He comes expectantly to the Lord to be forgiven and made pure. David cries out to God with a repentant heart, "Wash away all my iniquity and cleanse me from my sin" (Ps. 51:2). He lies prostrate before the Lord pleading for mercy, and trusting in the kindness of the Lord to make him pure again. "Cleanse me with hyssop, and I will be clean; wash me, and I will be whiter than snow" (Ps. 51:7). David must have appeared very undignified as royalty, but he demonstrated vulnerability.

Be vulnerable before those whom you lead. Leaders set the example for others. If you admit you have failed, others are more likely to follow your example. Confessing sin to others brings forgiveness and healing. It is tough for most all of us to admit we have failed.

One of my most vivid experiences of being vulnerable happened when I was a part of a leadership team for a women's retreat. God emphatically instructed me to admit my sin of too often looking lustfully at women. I tried to convince God to let me off the hook, but He insisted. Admitting this weakness before fifty women was a very humbling experience. But, after being vulnerable before them and my wife, I felt clean. From that point on, it has been easier to resist the temptation to gaze lustfully.

Purity is Essential

Hebrews 10:22-23 issues a call for all believers to preserve in faith: "Let us draw near to God with a sincere heart and in full assurance of faith, having our hearts sprinkled to cleanse us from a guilty conscience and having our bodies washed with pure water. Let us hold unswervingly to the hope we profess, for He who promised is faithful."

We cannot enter the presence of God on earth or in heaven if we are stained dark by sin. If we desire to draw near to God, we must do so with sincere and pure hearts. It is Jesus who enables us to draw near to God. He shed His blood on a cruel cross providing the one and only way to wash away our guilt. We are not pure, but our hands and hearts are washed clean by faith in Him. So, we hold unwaveringly to the blessed hope that as leaders He has made us new. Our hands and hearts are made clean every time we confess our sin!

You lead. Step up to repent and experience purity of heart!

CHAPTER 7: LEADERS SEEK WISDOM

God is wise and He is the only source of all wisdom. Outside of a personal relationship with the one true God of the universe, there is no wisdom. "The fear of the Lord is the beginning of knowledge, but fools despise wisdom and discipline" (Prov. 1:7).

We start an intimate relationship with God as we acknowledge our human inability to do what is right. Our choices and decisions always get us into trouble. As we turn in love to Him and learn to rely on Him, we experience His wisdom.

Spiritual leaders need God's gift of wisdom. We need it for our personal lives, and we need it to lead others effectively. Spiritual leaders use God's Word to guide our lives. Our deepest understanding of life, His will and His purposes for our lives come through studying Scripture. The Bible reveals who God is and how to live our lives best. As we read, the Holy Spirit reveals the heart of God to us, enabling us to enjoy an intimate relationship with Him.

Wisdom and Knowledge

Wisdom is not intuition. Every human may have quick and ready insight, especially in those areas where we are most experienced and comfortable. A mother has a sensitivity to her children that enables her to know and understand something about them which is unseen and unsubstantiated by her natural senses. A businessperson may have insight not authenticated by the numbers on the company reports. We may all have intuition.

Wisdom is radically different from intuition. Wisdom does not come from within every human being. True wisdom comes from God and is a gift He freely offers to us all in our intimate personal relationship with Him through Jesus. Jesus Christ is the "wisdom of God" (see 1 Cor.1:24). Wisdom comes as we seek and hear the voice of God.

Nikki Gumble, author, Anglican priest, and developer of the Alpha Course says, "Knowledge is horizontal, wisdom is vertical." Human beings partner with God to impart knowledge to one another, but only God offers the gift of wisdom.

Wisdom has untold value. Leaders cannot do without it. Proverbs 8:17-19 personifies wisdom, "I love those who love me, and those who seek me find me. With me are riches and honor, enduring wealth, and prosperity. My fruit is better than fine gold; what I yield surpasses choice silver."

Wisdom enables leaders to lead effectively. A strong leader needs common sense, but more than that, we need the gift of wisdom. "By me kings reign and rulers make laws that are just; by me princes govern, and all nobles who rule on earth" (Prov. 8:15-16).

Godly leaders view people through the eyes of wisdom, not their outward appearance. God sent Samuel to anoint the next king of Israel from among the sons of Jesse to replace King Saul. Samuel began looking at the outward appearance of the young men who stood before him. "But the Lord said to Samuel, 'Do not consider his appearance or his height, for I have rejected him. The Lord does not look at the things man looks at. Man looks at the outward appearance, but the Lord looks at the heart'" (1 Sam. 16:7).

Jesus, an incredible leader, looked at the heart. He viewed the prostitute, not from her outward appearance but her heart of love. Her experience of Jesus' unconditional forgiveness had filled her heart with love for Him and dramatically transformed her life (see Lk. 7:36-50).

The Evidence of Wisdom

To be truly wise is to walk with God obediently. Our wisdom is evident to everyone when we follow the Lord's leading. We are wise leaders when we go where God tells us to go and do what He tells us to do. Our daily walk with Him reflects His wisdom. We do what our Father does, and we speak what our Father speaks.

Jesus told a parable about the wise and the foolish in Matthew 7:24-27:

> Therefore everyone who hears these words of Mine and puts them into practice is like a wise man who built his house on the rock. The rain came down, the streams rose, and the winds blew and beat against that house, yet it did not fall, because it had its foundation on the rock. But everyone who hears these words of Mine and does not put them into practice is like a foolish man who built his house on sand. The rain came down, the streams rose, and the winds blew and beat against that house, and it fell with a great crash.

According to Jesus, wisdom is more than the knowledge we have stored in our brains. True wisdom goes beyond our educational experience and mentoring. The heart of true wisdom is learning to live our lives uniquely—setting ourselves apart from the rest by our unique behavior and distinctive lives. Wise leaders faithfully put Jesus' teaching into practice in their lives.

Wise leaders build their lives on the teachings of Jesus. Following His ways enables us to build our lives on the only solid foundation. When the terrible storms of life come, and the waters rise to drown us, we stand firm on our rock-solid foundation. Our house is not swept away by the flood waters. Our house does not fall when the rain pelts or the winds plummet. Nothing destroys the life of the wise person.

Foolish persons build their lives on shifting sands. We are foolish when we construct our lives on anything other than the Word of God. When the storms come with torrential rains and high winds, the life of the foolish person is in dire straits. The house of their lives is full of unresolved issues. It is weak and readily subject to sudden destruction.

Avoid Foolishness

The Christian leaders' guidebook has much to say about wisdom, with a considerable collection of material known as "wisdom literature." Throughout Scripture, we find references to foolishness, the antonym of wisdom.

At times, people whose stories are told in the Bible act foolishly. Some lament these wrong decisions and actions and even admit it is sinful (see 1 Sam. 26:21 and 1 Chr. 21:8).

I concluded some time ago that all sin is irrational. It just never makes sense to do the wrong things we do.

At first, I observed the sinful actions of others and would consistently think, "How foolish, why on earth would a person do such a thing. It just doesn't make sense." Then as God shined His light on my sin, I was forced to conclude that my sin was very foolish too. All sin is irrational and foolish.

The Bible frequently speaks of avoiding foolishness, the opposite of wisdom. We all make bad spontaneous decisions at times that make us look foolish. How do we avoid foolish actions?

One of the ways we resist making bad decisions is to purpose in our hearts to make wise decisions before getting into any situation. I learned this principle from the story of Daniel, Shadrach, Meshach and Abednego in Daniel 1.

The young Israelite captives learned they would be eating gourmet food and drinking wine from the king's royal table every day. "But Daniel resolved not to defile himself with the royal food and wine, and he asked the chief official for permission not to defile himself this way" (Dan. 1:8). His wise young friends joined him. The result of their resolve was they looked healthier and better nourished than all the rest.

I don't know about you, but I have difficulty daily making wise choices to eat the healthiest foods. I recognize my body is a temple of the Holy Spirit. I understand some foods harm my temple, especially when eaten in excess. I want to eat smaller portions to lose weight. I know how important it is to decrease the salt intake to lower my blood pressure and get off the medication. But I find myself most often groaning out the confession of the Apostle Paul; "I do not understand what I do. For what I want to do I do not do, but what I hate I do" (Rom. 7:15). Until I have purposed in my heart to make wiser choices, I continue to make the same bad decisions.

Another way we avoid foolishness is to learn to hold our tongues. Wisdom is most evident in our lives when we are silent. Many in our society are bent on sharing their opinions about anything and everything. Our television and social media outlets give all too abundant opportunity and freedom for anyone and everyone to express their views, no matter how ill-informed or ridiculous.

Ancient Scripture very accurately describes our world today. "A fool finds no pleasure in understanding but delights in airing his own opinions" (Prov. 18:2). God's Word rings true for us. "Even a fool is thought wise if he keeps silent, and discerning if he holds his tongue" (Prov. 17:28). It is unnecessary as a leader for you to express your opinion on every news report, current event, or celebrity decision. Stand boldly on your Christian convictions while keeping most of your personal opinions to yourself.

Spiritual leaders are not above nor exempt from foolish decisions. While serving as pastor to pastors, I was all too frequently disappointed by the foolishness of pastors. As I pastor, I am certainly sorry to have to admit that pastors are sometimes very foolish. One of my friends, who was a pastor to pastors lamented, "I think some of my pastors get up every morning and ask, 'What can I do today that is stupid?'"

Leaders can make foolish decisions which negatively affect the lives of many people. A pastor on my watch was charged with drinking and driving when he drove his car into the ditch. Another pastor caused deep division in his church when he sexually harassed several women in the church. A young married pastor slipped out in the middle of the night to the bed of the church secretary. Foolish decisions!

All Wisdom Is a Gift from God

I conclude where I began this chapter. Wisdom is a gift God offers to everyone who asks. The desire of King Solomon's heart was to have divine wisdom to lead his nation. God answered his prayer and added the blessings of peace and prosperity.

The first chapter of Daniel reveals how Daniel and his three friends experienced the favor of God when they received the gift of wisdom.

To these four young men, God gave knowledge and understanding of all kinds of literature and learning. And Daniel could understand visions and dreams of all kinds. At the end of the time set by the king to bring them in, the chief official presented them to Nebuchadnezzar. The king talked with them, and he found none equal to Daniel, Hananiah, Mishael and Azariah; so they entered the king's service. In every matter of wisdom and understanding about which the king questioned them, he found them ten times better than all the magicians and enchanters in his whole kingdom. (Daniel 1:17-20)

You can have wisdom whether you are in a position of leadership or not. James 1:5 affirms, "If any of you lacks wisdom, you should ask God, who gives generously to all without finding fault, and it will be given to him." Ask Him today.

You lead. Step up to seek wisdom!

CHAPTER 8: LEADERS FAIL

Every leader fails sometimes. Most of us fail frequently. You and I fail God, others and ourselves. We fail those who love and trust us the most. We never plan to fail. When we fail, we are often astounded, we cannot believe it has happened to us. We know other leaders fail, but not us. Leaders often mistakenly think, "It will never happen to me." We are human, and every human being fails. God's Word makes it very plain, "There is no difference, for all have sinned and fall short of the glory of God" (Rom. 3:22-23).

Admit Failure

It is always difficult for us to admit we have failed. We refuse to confess guilt. It is a rare experience in our modern courtrooms to hear anyone admit quilt. But the culture of heaven is radically different from the cultures of the earth. God instructs us to admit our guilt.

Confession is good for the soul. Confession of sin brings healing and wholeness. Listen to David sing his song expressing the joys of confession.

> Blessed is he
>   whose transgressions are forgiven,
>   whose sins are covered.
> Blessed is the man
>   whose sin the Lord does not count against him
>   and in whose spirit is no deceit.
> When I kept silent,
>   my bones wasted away
>   through my groaning all day long.
> For day and night
>   Your hand was heavy on me;
> my strength was sapped

> as in the heat of summer. Selah
> Then I acknowledged my sin to You
>   and did not cover up my iniquity.
> I said, "I will confess
>   my transgressions to the Lord."
> And You forgave
>   the guilt of my sin. (Psalm 32:1-4)

At first, David refused to admit he had failed God and others. He thought he was keeping his sin a secret. He believed no one knew and no one else experienced the effect of his failures. He, and he alone had been affected. Unacknowledged sin had made him physically, emotionally and spiritually ill. Our unacknowledged sin has the identical effect on us.

I picture David groaning in emotional and perhaps even physical pain. His physical strength and his emotional energy were depleted. Depression exhausted his desire to accomplish what the day and his duties required. The spiritual burden of the heavy hand of God weighed him down day after day.

Relief and refreshing rushed over David when he finally admitted, "I am guilty!" When he exposed his cover-up, he experienced great release in his spirit.

We experience God's forgiveness when we admit our guilt to Him. Hold tight to God's promise, "If we confess our sins, He is faithful and just and will forgive us our sins and purify us from all unrighteousness" (1 Jn. 1:9).

Seek Help

We often find it very challenging to admit our failures to others. But, admitting failure to others has a cathartic effect on our lives. "Therefore confess your sins to each other and pray for each other so that you may be healed. The prayer of a righteous man is powerful and effective" (Jas. 5:16). We are relieved of the effects of sin when we admit our guilt to other believers and ask them to petition God on our behalf.

Every leader needs trusted friends and confidantes who will walk alongside us. "Walk with the wise and become wise, for a companion of fools suffers harm" (Prov. 13:20). These mentors help keep us accountable for the decisions we make and the actions we take. We need persons we can trust to keep our confession confidential. Not everyone can be trusted to have our best interests at heart.

We need friends we can count on to pick us up when we fall. Ecclesiastes 4:9-10 declares, "Two are better than one, because they have a good return for their work: If one falls down, his friend can help him up. But pity the man who falls and has no one to help them up!"

My wife, Marcia is my closest friend and confidante. She, more than any person in this world, is aware of my failures and sin. I count her as the richest blessing from God in my life. I can never question the goodness and favor of God in my life when I look at her. She has helped me many times to confess sin first to God and then to her. Her love helps hold me accountable to God and to those I lead. Whenever I have fallen, she has never failed to help me up. Her record of faithfulness is amazing, considering we have been married for over forty years now!

Some time ago I discovered the need also to have male friends who help to hold me accountable. I meet on a regular basis, usually once a week with a male prayer partner. We openly share our joys, sorrows, struggles, and pain. We pray for one another and experience the Lord's promised healing. Our time together is centered on James 5:16. We hold one another accountable as we pray. We seek God's answers and help when we have failed. We long for His wisdom to lead and guide us most effectively. We strive to partner with God and with each other to advance the Kingdom of God on earth.

Learn from Your Mistakes

I don't always learn from my mistakes, but when I do, it is usually significant and long-lasting. Early in my ministry, I served as associate pastor of a fifteen-hundred-member congregation where I had oversight of the youth ministry. I was responsible for recruiting, training and overseeing adult volunteers for the youth department.

A man who had served time in prison began to be involved in the life of the church. After an adult volunteer had invited him to speak to the youth group, he began to volunteer with the youth group for a few weeks. Concerned parents of our youth contacted the attorney general of our state to inquire about the reason our new volunteer had been in prison. When they learned, they became outraged, demanding his immediate removal as a volunteer with the youth group. I agreed that under the circumstances he should not be directly involved with youth.

Our senior pastor had ministered to the man for some time and had come to know him well. He and I both trusted the man and earnestly believed he had truly repented and was a changed person. I felt as Christians we were called to forgive him and offer him the opportunity to have a fresh start in life. Several of the parents were not ready to forgive so quickly. So, our senior pastor and I sat down with the man to tell him he could no longer volunteer with our youth group.

My mistake in the situation was to refuse to forgive the parents who would not forgive him. My unforgiving attitude burned inside me. I avoided the people I refused to forgive. I was angry and well on my way to bitterness for a couple of months. In one of my weekly church newsletter articles, I broached the subject of forgiveness. I merely quoted, without comment, the story of Jesus' response to the woman caught in the act of adultery in John 8:1-11.

Later that week my parents had come from North Carolina to visit us in Kentucky. I had worked diligently to recruit enough volunteers for a Saturday event for children so I could show up, help get the morning started and leave to spend quality time with my parents. By the end of the week, several of the volunteers had schedule conflicts, leaving me with the responsibility. So, I began Saturday morning already extremely frustrated.

I was exasperated when I received a phone call at the church from a woman who was concerned about the situation of this youth volunteer, recently released from prison. She didn't have children or grandchildren in the youth group. As far as I was concerned it just wasn't any of her business. She complained that she and others believed I directed my newsletter article at them. Anger rose in me. In a manner quite uncharacteristic of me, I quickly and poignantly replied, "If the shoe fits, wear it!" I felt I could have bitten a ten-penny nail in two. My anger at the situation and the people involved ignited at a new level of intensity.

Easter was only a few days away when God began to soften my heart. I knew I could not celebrate the resurrection of Jesus until I had dealt with my unforgiveness. It was eating me alive inside. So, I decided to go to talk to each of the three families whom I had avoided and had refused to forgive.

Early the Saturday morning before Easter, I went unannounced first to the home of the lady who had no one in the youth group with the intention of repenting and asking her to forgive me. She opened the door of her home with one hand and opened her arms to receive me with a big hug before I uttered a single word. She graciously welcomed me into her home. It was apparent she was not angry with me at all. When I repeatedly tried to convince her that I was sorry and to ask her forgiveness, she just didn't let me do it. She was not upset or angry with me at all. She had something else of greater priority on her mind.

She and her husband had learned a few days before our phone conversation he had kidney cancer. They told me he had been born with only one kidney, and now his only kidney had a fully involved malignancy. They had not yet informed anyone from the church or staff about this heartbreaking news.

I learned from the mistake of unforgiveness. First, I realized how detrimental unforgiveness could be emotionally and spiritually. My refusal to forgive in this experience did not hurt others, but it burned like a fire inside me. I lived night and day with the slow, steady destruction of peace in my heart and life.

I had even regressed to a behavior of my childhood. As a teenager when I was angry with my parents I usually didn't take it out on them but directed my anger at the basketball court in our yard. I dribbled the ball hard; ran as fast as possible, and fired the ball at the goal. I lifted my five-foot-six-inch frame as high as I possibly could in a vain attempt to dunk the basketball in anger. All to no avail, of course. Except, I didn't get in further trouble with my parents by being disrespectful to them. Now, as an adult, I didn't have a basketball or goal available. So, I went for long walks, and childishly threw rocks at trees in anger.

I learned another valuable lesson from the situation. Very often when people respond in ways that are uncharacteristic of them, they are reacting out of pain in some area of their lives. Their response to us may have little if anything to do with what is happening in our relationship with them.

That Saturday morning experience marked the beginning of a very profound and meaningful relationship with the lady and her husband. Over the next few months, as her husband's health deteriorated, I was privileged to be there with them. My family and I were in their home frequently. I visited and prayed with them every time he went to the hospital. It was an honor when she asked me to help lead his funeral service. Then one year to the day after her husband's death her only son committed suicide. I was the first person she called. She invited me to assist in leading his funeral service.

Learn from your mistakes. Don't make the same mistakes twice. I want to seek God's discernment consistently. I desire the wisdom to discover how to relate to everyone in a healthy manner, especially with those persons the Lord has entrusted to my leadership and care.

Know You Are Not Disqualified

When someone fails us, we humans often reject them. Even people we value highly are written off in our books if they fail us if only one time. But God did not reject David as the leader even though he had broken two of God's own Ten Commandments: "You shall not commit adultery:" (Ex. 20:14), and "You shall not murder" (Ex. 20:13). God's forgiveness is incredible, isn't it!

God unconditionally loved and forgave King David. He was not disqualified as a leader even though he miserably failed God at a very base level. God chose David to lead as king, but David did not live up to God's expectations of all His followers. Notice, however, God did not remove David from his position of leadership. David remained King of Israel with the blessing of God because he was willing to confess his failure. We are not disqualified as leaders by God if we acknowledge our inability and guilt. God forgives.

We experience divine forgiveness when we confess our sin. But, the consequences of our bad choices continue. I believe God often shows mercy in such a way that He reduces the effects of sin when we confess. However, He never eliminates the consequences entirely.

We can never thwart God's divine law of reaping and sowing. We reap what we sow. Like David, we will suffer the consequences of our sin. David's son by Bathsheba died. Violence and calamity in his household filled his reign as king. His son, Absalom, led a coup against him. David reaped what he had sown, but he was never disqualified and declared as unfit by God. You and I are not disqualified and declared unfit for service when we fail if we truly repent!

Experience God's Forgiveness

No matter how miserably we have failed God, He is willing to forgive. He does not count our sin and failure against us. In fact, His forgiveness is thorough and complete. When we confess our sin, He even forgets that it ever happened.

So far as I have been able to determine from studying Scripture, the only thing Almighty God forgets is the sin we have confessed. He does not forget us (see Is. 49:15). He never forgets His covenant promises (see Deut. 4:31). But, God does forget our sin when we confess it. "I, even I, am He who blots out your transgressions, for My own sake, *and remembers your sins no more*" (Is. 43:25, emphasis mine).

Throughout most of my life, I have understood and experienced God's forgiveness for the sins I committed when I repented. I knew if I confessed my willful disobedience and rebellion God was quick to forgive. But, I served as pastor for many years before I believed God forgave me when I failed Him in ministry.

I experienced guilt when I was unable to accomplish the goals I had set for my day. If I didn't visit someone who was sick, comfort someone who was grieving, help someone in need or do any sermon preparation, I felt guilty. It was the guilt over my sins of omission that I carried with me. And I believed those sins were many.

From my perspective, a pastor's work is never done. I could never lay my head on my pillow at night and rejoice believing I had accomplished everything that needed to be done that day. There was always more to do.

I now experience God's forgiveness for sins of omission. I know He forgives when I don't produce the fruit He knows I can create when I join Him in what He is doing. When I repent for my failure to meet His expectations in my ministry, I know He forgives.

Peter boldly and boastfully promised Jesus he would never deny Jesus even if it meant he had to die (see Matt. 26:31-34). But that same evening after Jesus was arrested Peter denied even knowing Jesus three times. When the rooster crowed, Peter recalled Jesus' prediction of his denial. He ran outside in shame. Heartbroken, he wept bitterly (see Matt. 26:75).

Peter experienced the forgiving love of Jesus a few days later (see Jn. 21:15-19). God raised Jesus from the dead. As He appeared to His disciples for the third time He questioned Peter, "Peter, do you love me?" Peter affirmed His love for Jesus each time Jesus asked the question. Peter must have been elated when Jesus' forgiveness became real, and Jesus reinstated him to his ministry as a disciple. Our Lord forgives us when we fail Him today.

You lead. Step up to overcome your failures!

CHAPTER 9: LEADERS CONFRONT OPPOSITION

Jesus did not retreat in the face of opposition. He met it head-on with the authority that belonged to Him as the Son of God. Satan opposed Jesus in the wilderness temptation. Jesus did not back down from His archenemy. He stood face to face, nose to nose, toe to toe, with no fear.

On several occasions, the leaders of the religious establishment confronted Jesus. Those confrontations increased as the time of Jesus' death rapidly approached. They questioned His authority on many occasions. Matthew 21:23 records one incident:

> Jesus entered the temple courts, and, while he was teaching, the chief priests and the elders of the people came to him. 'By what authority are you doing these things?' they asked. 'And who gave you this authority?'" The religious leaders questioned Jesus' authority to teach, to heal, to forgive sin, and refute their interpretation of the law.

Every leader faces this type of opposition. Expect your authority to be challenged. Children call the authority of their parents into question. Most young children earnestly believe and often declare that their parents are smarter and stronger than everyone else. But wait until those same little darlings have been in school two or three years. You may no longer be the most intelligent person in their lives. You hear them declare, "My teacher said it" (so it is most certainly correct). In the mind of your child, your parental authority has diminished. If your experience is like that of many parents, your authority will be challenged to a much greater measure when your child becomes a teenager.

The authority of employers, law enforcement officers, teachers, pastors, political leaders and business leaders are all challenged in our world. What are we to do when faced with the challenges of opposition?

As a leader today, I want to follow Jesus' example when faced with opposition that questions my authority. Jesus did not flaunt His power over anyone. He did not defend Himself when His authority was called into question. The Lord did not enter debate or argument concerning His authority. He knew who He was and He stood without wavering on the truth.

Instead of defending His authority, He only asked pointed, direct questions. Instead of talking about who He was, He demonstrated His power with action on behalf of others. For example, the Gospel of Luke records an incident where Jesus' authority to forgive sin was questioned.

> "Which is easier: to say, 'Your sins are forgiven,' or to say, 'Get up and walk'? But that you may know that the Son of Man has authority on earth to forgive sins...' He said to the paralyzed man, 'I tell you, get up, take your mat and go home.' Immediately he stood up in front of them, took what he had been lying on and went home praising God. (Luke 5:23-25)

It was not so much the words He spoke, but the action Jesus took that demonstrated and proved His authority time after time. When we are confident in our authority as leaders, we will act to show it in a manner that transforms the lives of others. Jesus never made authority about Himself.

Many leaders make the mistake of thinking authority is for our benefit instead of the interests of others. Many gifted leaders have fallen because they abused authority. Many leaders have bought into the entitlement mentality, "I earned this or I deserve this as a person in authority." The result of this attitude is often stealing from the company, lavish living through deceptive practices, verbal and sexual abuse of employees, the abuse of power or a combination of these. From the Christian perspective, authority is never intended to give leaders greater rights or privileges. Authority comes instead with greater responsibility.

Opposition arose against Jesus as His theology was frequently called into question. The religious leaders of His day did not believe many of the things Jesus taught about God. Jesus knew God created the Sabbath for human beings. But, the religious leaders wanted to make keeping the Sabbath a law that separated people from the love of God.

> Going on from that place, He went into their synagogue, and a man with a shriveled hand was there. Looking for a reason to accuse Jesus, they asked Him, "Is it lawful to heal on the Sabbath?" He said to them, "If any of you has a sheep and it falls into a pit on the Sabbath, will you not take hold of it and lift it out? How much more valuable is a man than a sheep! Therefore it is lawful to do good on

the Sabbath." Then He said to the man, "Stretch out your hand." So he stretched it out and it was completely restored, just as sound as the other. But the Pharisees went out and plotted how they might kill Jesus. (Matthew 12:9-14)

What you believe about God will be called into question at times. Your theology will be opposed. Be very careful as a spiritual leader to keep your faith firmly grounded in God's Word.

How will you, a spiritual leader, respond when your faith is questioned?

Jesus stood firm on His convictions. He always demonstrated love for people. The letter of the human-made law was not Jesus' priority but rather His love for people. He revealed that His love for the man with the withered hand took precedence over the law. He confronted opposition to His theology with a demonstration of love.

The identity of Jesus was called into question from the very beginning of His ministry. God, the Father, affirmed Jesus as His very own Son at His baptism. "And a voice from heaven said, 'This is My Son, whom I love; with Him I am well pleased'" (Matt. 3:17).

The wilderness temptations immediately questioned His identity. Satan challenged twice, "If you are the Son of God…" Jesus met both challenges as He declared His convictions based on the Word of God.

As leaders, it is imperative that we know who we are. Know your identity. Know who you are in Christ. Stand boldly on the Word of God. You, too, are a child of God. 1 John 3:1 declares the truth, "How great is the love the Father has lavished on us, that we should be called children of God! And that is what we are!"

Nehemiah Confronted Opposition

Nehemiah was a gifted leader whose story we find in the Bible. He is an excellent example of a leader who faced and overcame opposition. We can glean leadership principles from Nehemiah that will equip us to confront and overcome opposition.

Seek the Lord (see Neh. 1)

Christian leaders must seek the Lord in all we do. When faced with opposition the key to challenging and overcoming it is our relationship with God. Seek His face and His wisdom.

In Babylon, Nehemiah learned his country was in dire straits. The walls of the capital city of Jerusalem were broken down and its' gates burned. Heartbroken, his first response was to cry out and seek help from the King of the Universe. In humility, Nehemiah was convinced that the restoration of his nation was impossible without the intervention of Almighty God. He knew from the depths of his heart he could not do it alone.

Nehemiah wept when he learned of the plight of his homeland. Though grief-stricken, he experienced the call of God to be a part of the solution. Nehemiah began to seek the face of God. He admitted he and his people were in this tragic predicament due to their past failures, sins, and bad decisions. He cried out for personal and national forgiveness. He asked the Lord for favor with the king to leave his post as cupbearer to return to his homeland. His heart's desire was to lead his people to rebuild Jerusalem and partner with God to transform the nation.

If you are facing opposition today, you need the Holy Spirit to guide you into all truth. He will give you the wisdom to confront opposition. Seek the Lord. You may hear other voices clamoring for your attention, claiming to have the answers you seek. Listen to the Lord's wise voice. Place your trust fully and completely in Him.

Stand Courageously on Your God-given authority (see Neh. 2)

King Artaxerxes trusted Nehemiah, his cupbearer, to protect and serve him. The king had granted Nehemiah authority in his household and his kingdom. In the beginning, Nehemiah was uncertain of the level of his power. We quickly learn Nehemiah enjoyed the favor of the king. He put the king's support to the test when he hesitantly requested help from him.

King Artaxerxes graciously granted Nehemiah favor and confirmed Nehemiah's authority by sending letters for protection to travel through potentially hostile territory and for provision to rebuild the city walls. Nehemiah must have been surprised when the king went beyond his requests to send a military escort to accompany him. The king granted much more than Nehemiah asked or expected!

As Christians, we have God-given authority. Authority as children of the King is given to us the moment we place our trust in Jesus. We have greater authority in His Kingdom than we often realize or accept. Christ invites us to stand courageously knowing we are the children of the King of the universe. There is no greater authority than God's authority, and He has given it to us!

Confront Opposition with the Truth (see Neh. 2:10-20)

Opposition arose against the Lord and His servant, Nehemiah, before he even arrived in Jerusalem. This external opposition began with Sanballat and Tobiah, kings of the enemies of Israel (see Nehemiah 2:10). As is so often true today, the opponents of Israel convinced others to ally with them. In Nehemiah 2:19 a third nation, led by King Gesham, the Arab, opposed Israel's rebuilding the country.

The moment the leaders of the remnant of the nation agreed to start rebuilding the walls of Jerusalem, the enemies of Israel intensified their interference by mocking and ridiculing. "But when Sanballat the Horonite,

Tobiah the Ammonite official and Geshem the Arab heard about it, they mocked and ridiculed us. 'What is this you are doing?' they asked. 'Are you rebelling against the king?'" (Neh. 2:19).

Nehemiah faced this opposition from the mocking kings head-on by speaking the truth. To paraphrase, he declared, "You have no authority, no claim, or right to speak concerning our nation" (see Neh. 2:20). Notice Nehemiah did not run, hide, or ignore the opposition. He confronted them with the truth.

Nehemiah purposed in his heart that he would not be distracted from fulfilling the desire of his heart and the resolve of the leaders of his nation. His response to the opposition was brief and to the point. He didn't waste time or dignify their mocking with the retorts they must have expected. He didn't mince words, "This is not your business." Notice, he knew the truth was on his side, so he did not even mention the king's letter of affirmation when the enemies of his nation accused him of leading an insurrection against the king.

"I answered them by saying, 'The God of heaven will give us success. We His servants will start rebuilding, but as for you, you have no share in Jerusalem or any claim or historic right to it'" (Neh. 2:20).

Leaders today experience opposition of this nature. The opposition takes the form of lies, often from the mouths of people who have no authority or position in the entity they badmouth. It was a lie that Nehemiah was rebelling against the king. He did, in fact, have the written permission of the king (and the call of God) to do what he was leading the people to do.

Sanballat and Tobiah had no business in the business of Nehemiah and Jerusalem. They were foreigners looking in on the decisions of a nation not their own.

Have you been faced with opposition from someone outside your sphere of rightful influence? What response is appropriate? Nehemiah's response was to begin by reasoning with those who had no business or authority in the life of his people. But, his response was brief and matter-of-fact, so he was not distracted from the vision.

Stay Focused on the Vision (see Neh. 3-4)

Nehemiah's God-given vision was to rebuild the walls of Jerusalem and restore the nation. Nehemiah led the remnant of Israel to develop a strategy for rebuilding the walls of the city. Clans and people groups each rebuilt the section of the walls and the city gates in their neighborhood. The people zealously embraced the vision and the arduous physical labor. In a short time, half the walls were reconstructed.

If you have a great vision, you will certainly be distracted by the opposition. It is not only external opponents who distract us from fulfilling our vision. The practical, day to day aspects of life quickly sidetrack us. I am distracted from my vision to write this book by the need to complete my self-imposed portion of household chores. Making a bed, washing breakfast dishes or throwing in a load of laundry are all practical and necessary parts of everyday life. But, the vision must be the priority. I have the leisure of setting my schedule as to when I complete these tasks.

As leaders, we are often distracted by good things that prevent us from accomplishing the best God has for us. These diversions are not wrong or evil. Although they cannot truthfully be identified as opponents or enemies, these practical tasks often sidetrack us from our higher vision and calling.

Do Not Defend Yourself (see Neh. 4)

The people of Israel were well on their way to fulfilling the vision. With half the Jerusalem city wall rebuilt, it was at this crucial time that the scoffing and ridicule from their enemies increased (see Nehemiah 4:1-3).

Notice there is no response from Nehemiah nor the leaders of Israel except to petition God for His help. There are no retaliatory insults, no threats of revenge and no bantering mockery. In fact, the leaders and the workers focused on the vision as they worked with all their hearts.

There comes a time when leaders refuse to listen to the mocking and ridicule, even when threats are real and imminent. There is a time to be silent. There comes a time when debate and retaliatory comments are counter-productive.

Jesus set the example for us when at His mock trials, He spoke not a word in defense. He had already confronted those who stood in opposition to Him with the truth. He challenged them with wise teaching and with a life of service on behalf of others. The fact that His Father's favor and power rested on Him was evident to everyone who encountered Him.

There is a time to be still and trust God to defend. Godly leaders join the Psalmist as he calls on the Lord: "Defend my cause and redeem me; preserve my life according to Your promise" (Ps. 119:154).

I saw this biblical leadership principle practiced powerfully in the life of a leader I deeply respect. While serving as the Madisonville District Superintendent of the United Methodist Church in Kentucky, Bishop James King and I were confronted with the most challenging experience in my ministry. We gathered in the sanctuary to inform the people of the church of indiscretions on the part of their pastor.

As is so often true, the congregation was divided on whether they believed the allegations. Those who refused to accept the truth become adamant and defensive. Tempers flared, and insults were publicly hurled at Bishop King. People who were ordinarily kind accused us of lying and trying to turn the church against their pastor.

What I witnessed on the part of my mentor, Bishop King, was amazing.

He did not speak a single word in his own defense. Bishop King demonstrated the same kind of forgiving attitude as Jesus on the cross when He uttered, "Father, forgive them, for they do not know what they are doing" (Lk. 23:34). Because there was no attempt on Bishop King's part to defend or retaliate with words or actions, I believe as leaders we experienced divine protection that day. We knew God was faithful to His promise to us and others who trust Him,

> When you pass through the waters,
>   I will be with you;
> and when you pass through the rivers,
>   they will not sweep over you.
> When you walk through the fire,
>   you will not be burned;
> the flames will not set you ablaze. (Isaiah 43:2)

Encourage and Challenge the People You Lead (see Neh. 4)

The enemies of Israel became incensed with anger when they learned the rebuilding had progressed far beyond their expectations. With half the wall restored they declared war on Israel and planned an attack on Jerusalem.

Nehemiah's laser focus on the vision and strategy is evident here. He vigorously issued the challenge to the leaders, laborers and the army to stand firm. As their leader, he bolstered their resolve and their courage to take a faith-filled position. He called out their faith to trust The Leader to protect them and to fight for them.

> After I looked things over, I stood up and said to the nobles, the officials and the rest of the people, "Don't be afraid of them. Remember the Lord, who is great and awesome, and fight for your brothers, your sons and your daughters, your wives and your homes." (Nehemiah 4:14)

History is replete with great leaders who stood boldly to inspire and encourage their followers to rise to the occasion. John F. Kennedy's inaugural address included this famous quotation, "And so, my fellow Americans, ask not what your country can do for you--ask what you can do for your country."

Patrick Henry stood before the Second Virginia Convention held at St. John's Church in Richmond, Virginia calling for armed resistance to England's political and military advances. His rousing patriotic speech ended with these words:

It is in vain, sir, to extenuate the matter. Gentlemen may cry, Peace, Peace, but there is no peace. The war is begun! The next gale that sweeps from the north will bring to our ears the clash of resounding arms! Our brethren are already in the field! Why stand we here idle? What is it that gentlemen wish? What would they have? Is life so dear, or peace so sweet, as to be purchased at the price of chains and slavery? Forbid it, Almighty God! I know not what course others may take; but as for me, give me liberty or give me death!" (Wirt, William. Sketches of the Life and Character of Patrick Henry (Philadelphia) 1836, as reproduced in The World's Great Speeches, Lewis Copeland and Lawrence W. Lamm, eds., (New York) 1973)

David was incensed when the giant Goliath defied the terrified armies of the living God for forty days (see 1 Samuel 17). As a shepherd boy with no experience as a soldier, he accepted the seasoned warrior, Goliath's challenge for one man to fight him. David shouted to Goliath as they stood poised to fight in the presence of the Philistine and Israelite armies. "All those gathered here will know that it is not by sword or spear that the Lord saves; for the battle is the Lord's, and He will give all of you into our hands" (1 Sam. 17:47).

God instructed Moses to send one leader from each of the twelve tribes to explore the land of Canaan and spy on the people there to determine their numbers and strength. Ten of the leaders returned to declare that the inhabitants of the land were more numerous and stronger than the people of Israel. Numbers 14:6-9 records the inspiring words of two great leaders,

Joshua son of Nun and Caleb son of Jephunneh, who were among those who had explored the land, tore their clothes and said to the entire Israelite assembly, "The land we passed through and explored is exceedingly good. If the Lord is pleased with us, He will lead us into that land, a land flowing with milk and honey, and will give it to us. Only do not rebel against the Lord. And do not be afraid of the people of the land, because we will swallow them up. Their protection is gone, but the Lord is with us. Do not be afraid of them."

Of the twelve spies, only Joshua and Caleb were ready to lead the people into battle. It is worthy here to note that the names of the other ten leaders although listed in the pages of Scripture are virtually unknown. Joshua and Caleb are household names among Christians.

Great leaders issue great challenges. John F. Kennedy, Patrick Henry, David, Joshua, and Caleb were all great leaders who issued great challenges. Every one of these leaders graphically articulated their messages of hope and their calls to trust and action. Every one of them not only expressed their willingness to put their lives on the line but proved their devotion to the people they led by running bravely onto the battlefields.

Readily Revise Your Strategy (see Neh. 4)

It may be necessary to alter your strategy to accomplish your vision and to protect the people you lead. Nehemiah learned how the enemy had multiplied insults, derision, and ridicule. But the people of Israel had poured heart and soul into the work so that the Jerusalem wall was restored to half its height (see Nehemiah 4:6). With the threat of a military attack on the city by a coalition of enemies uncovered, Nehemiah revised the strategy to meet this imminent danger.

The response of Nehemiah and the leaders of Israel was to pray for the Lord's protection and to enhance security by posting guards around their city. Night and day half of the men served as armed guards to watch over the builders. The material transporters held their weapons in one hand while they worked with the other hand. Every builder wore his sword on his belt (see Neh. 4:16-18).

This revised strategy slowed the work. It was harder to carry a weapon in one hand and building materials in the other. Half of the already weary workforce left their labor to provide the necessary security. Without this strategy revision, the project would fail.

The approach you take to confront opposition will determine whether you can fulfill God's vision for your life. If your focus is entirely on the opposition, you will fail to see God's possibilities. If you retaliate with insults and personal attacks, you will lose face in your own camp. If you seek revenge you will become bitter and so entranced you will soon lose sight of the vision.

Keep your eyes on Jesus and the prize He has set before you. Resolve with the Apostle Paul to reach the goal:

> Not that I have already obtained all this, or have already been made perfect, but I press on to take hold of that for which Christ Jesus took hold of me. Brothers, I do not consider myself yet to have taken hold of it. But one thing I do: Forgetting what is behind and straining toward what is ahead, I press on toward the goal to win the prize for which God has called me heavenward in Christ Jesus. (Philippians 3:12-14)

You lead. Step up to overcome opposition!

GARY D. BALL

CHAPTER 10: LEADERS RESOLVE CONFLICT

God's highest priority is His relationship with every human being He created. His heart's desire is that we have an intimate, personal relationship with Him. Jesus is the open door to engage in a personal relationship with the Father. Enter today into a personal relationship by stepping through the door. It is a gift we don't earn, work for, or deserve.

We are sinful by nature. Our sin offends God. But He has provided a way for our offenses to be erased and forgotten. Our Father sent His Son Jesus to pay the penalty for our sin. Ours is simply to trust, to admit we are guilty of sin against Him and to ask His forgiveness. "If we confess our sins, He is faithful and just and will forgive us our sins and purify us from all unrighteousness" (1 Jn. 1:9). We can live righteous lives before our Father, because of Jesus.

God has revealed that our second priority is our relationship with others. "And this is His command: to believe in the name of His Son, Jesus Christ, and to love one another as He commanded us" (1 Jn. 3:23).

The major roadblocks to maintaining a right relationship with others are offense and conflict. They will certainly come. As human beings, we cannot escape it. We offend, and we are offended. The question becomes, as leaders, what will we do with it? "He who covers over an offense promotes love, but whoever repeats the matter separates close friends" (Prov. 17:9).

Four Practical Steps

In Matthew 18:15-17, Jesus gives us clear, practical, down-to-earth guidance—four specific spiritual steps to deal with conflict and offense: Go alone to talk to the person who offended you. If he/she doesn't listen, take one or two others along with you. If the person still doesn't listen, take it to the church. If he refuses to listen to the church, treat him as you would treat a pagan.

First Practical Step: Go Alone to the Person Who Offended You

This action is the first and most important step. Even Christian leaders often refuse to do as Jesus instructed. Instead, we go first to other people to spew out on them how we have been offended. We frequently make mountains out of molehills.

Let's break down Jesus' instruction phrase by phrase: "If your brother sins against you, go and show him his fault just between the two of you. If he listens to you, you have won your brother over" (Matt. 18:15).

1. Access Carefully

Jesus said, "If"... "If your brother sins against you..." We start with the questions we must ask ourselves: Has this person actually sinned against me? Am I thinking only of myself, my desires, and my needs? Am I taking on the offenses of others? Am I too sensitive?

2. Pray Urgently

What does the Lord see in this situation? Ask Him earnestly, "Lord, how do you access this situation?" Listen intently for His response. Ask God to intervene, to soften the heart of the other person. Seek His help to know what you need to say. Ask Him to enable you to precisely articulate what you need to speak in love. Listen carefully for the Lord to speak to you.

3. Act Quickly

"Go and show him his fault..." We hate confrontation. Fear and hesitancy cause us to be passive, so we procrastinate. We become inactive, and wallow in the mud of self-pity. We go, but not to the person who has offended us. We run to tell other people. What does God's Word teach us about that?

"Do not let any unwholesome talk come out of your mouths, but only what is helpful for building others up according to their needs, that it may benefit those who listen" (Eph. 4:29).

I paraphrase this verse with what I consider to be a wholesome country expression: "If you can't say something good, don't say anything at all." We are challenged to build others up according to their needs.

Notice the following admonition: "And do not grieve the Holy Spirit..." (Eph. 4:30) Understand what the Lord is speaking in this context. To gossip, to slander, or to talk about how someone has offended us, grieves the Holy Spirit of God.

Too often we get angry. The more we speak, the angrier we get. We get angry, and we sin. "In your anger do not sin": do not let the sun go down while you are still angry, and do not give the devil a foothold" (Eph. 4:26-27).

Settle it quickly. Don't open the door for evil to enter.

"Get rid of all bitterness, rage and anger, brawling and slander, along with every form of malice. Be kind and compassionate to one another, forgiving each other, just as in Christ God forgave you" (Eph. 4:31-32).

Act quickly—purposing in your heart to forgive the person. Speak only to the one who has offended you.

4. Speak Truthfully

"Go and show him his fault..." If we are truly offended, it is dishonest to refuse to confront. Don't carry offenses. Be truthful with yourself and with those who have offended you.

Forgiveness is not saying the offense is nothing, is not real, or does not matter to us. Forgiveness confronts the truth. To ignore the issue is to be dishonest. It seems it is in our human nature to ignore persons who offend us. But, all the time the hurt festers inside. The poison of offense, hate, bitterness and backbiting builds inside us. Our physical body, our soul, and our spirit become toxic. Be careful to speak only the truth to the person who has offended you.

5. Offer Forgiveness

This principle is not found in Jesus' words in this passage, but it is certainly found in the teachings of Jesus and throughout the New Testament.

Why offer forgiveness? We groan, "It is their fault, their sin, their disrespect and their disregard for us. Why would I offer forgiveness? Besides, they have not asked for my forgiveness. They have not admitted their fault."

There are many reasons to offer forgiveness:

One, God created us in His image. God forgives. It is His nature to forgive. He created us with the power to forgive. He always enables us to forgive when it is in our hearts.

Two, we are commanded to forgive. "And when you stand praying, if you hold anything against anyone, forgive him, so that your Father in heaven may forgive you your sins" (Mk. 11:25).

Three, if we refuse to forgive, we forfeit His forgiveness. This consequence of failing to forgive is not the church's idea; it is God's principle. "For if you forgive men when they sin against you, your heavenly Father will also forgive you. But if you do not forgive men their sins, your Father will not forgive your sins" (Matt. 6:14-15).

Four, we forgive and God heals us. Unforgiveness poisons our spirit and soul. Unforgiveness is to the spirit what gangrene is to the physical body. Unforgiveness infects our whole person. We have discovered in healing ministry that unforgiveness is at the root of several physical diseases and illnesses. Forgiveness releases God's healing physically, emotionally, spiritually and relationally.

Five, we experience much forgiveness. We find Jesus' parable of the unforgiving servant in Matthew 18:21-35. Jesus is prompted to tell this parable by Peter's question, "How many times am I to forgive someone who offends me?"

"Seven times?" Peter questions. Peter's understanding that seven is the perfect number meant if he forgave seven offenses that he could then refuse to forgive again because he would have already forgiven perfectly. Jesus answered, "Seventy-seven times."

Jesus' point is to forgive more times than we can keep a record. Forgive anyone who offends us on an endless number of occasions. Take no offense!

In response to Peter, Jesus begins to tell a parable about a king who sets out to settle his accounts. One servant owes an enormous debt. There was no way he could pay. He begins to plead for mercy, but instead, the king offers grace. He decided to cancel the servant's debt. He wrote "paid in full" across the face of the bill. The man's debt is fully forgiven.

The King took no offense. But that same servant acted with unforgiveness and cruelty. He refused to forgive a small debt owed him by a fellow servant. He showed no mercy. He extended no grace. The end of the story is that the servant was punished severely for unforgiveness. The king then refused to forgive when his servant was unwilling to forgive.

6. Maintain Confidentiality

"Go and show him his fault, just between the two of you" (Matt. 18:15). Resolving offenses must be kept confidential. When we "share" how we have been offended by others we are only passing along gossip.

If we tell others how we have been offended, it is contagious. The poison spreads to the mind and hearts of others. Others are hesitant now to trust the person involved. Others guard their relationship with them. Others think less of the person than before. Others often take on our offenses, making them their own.

Be careful to keep your conversation confidential. Don't talk about it before you go to the person who offended you. Don't talk about it after you go to them.

7. Wait Patiently

"If he listens to you…" (Matt.18:15). Once you have truthfully informed the person who offended you, you have done what God expects in the first step. The ball is now in their court. You have no control over their decision. God does not promise to take control of their response. He gives them free will to listen to you, admit their fault, sin or injustice, ask for your forgiveness and be reconciled. Or, they can refuse to listen, deny the truth and offend you again. There is always risk involved when we obey God.

God's desire always is forgiveness. He will guide you as you go to speak the truth. He will work in the heart of the person who has offended you. If your plea for reconciliation is cast aside, continue to pray.

8. Celebrate Joyfully

"If he listens to you, you have won your brother over" (Matt. 18:15).

God's desire and goal is always to heal relationships. It is His will always to bring reconciliation. You will always have His help when you take this approach. Always! Celebrate reconciliation!

Second Practical Step: Take One or Two Others with You

The person who offended you may refuse God's help for them. "But if he will not listen, take one or two others along, so that 'every matter may be established by the testimony of two or three witnesses'" (Matt. 18:16).

It is important to take someone with you because it is a primary principle of the law of God. "One witness is not enough to convict a man accused of any crime or offense he may have committed. A matter must be established by the testimony of two or three witnesses" (see Deut. 19:15).

Only one or two other people are to be made aware of the situation. Other people are now involved as mediators and as witnesses on behalf of the individual who has been offended. It is vital to choose believers gifted at reconciliation and who can be trusted to keep the conversation confidential. We are to make a concerted effort to resolve the conflict in this setting.

Seek God's guidance, ask Him who you should take with you. Do not take someone with you who is carrying your offense. Take a person who carries peace and a heart for reconciliation. Walk through the same steps as when you went alone. If the individual who has offended you still refuses to listen, continue to do as Jesus instructed.

Third Practical Step: Tell It to the Church

"If he refuses to listen to them, tell it to the church" (Matt. 18:17). It is not until the third attempt at reconciliation on the part of a believer that the matter becomes public knowledge. Even then it is only the church that is to learn about the situation. I believe it is Jesus' expectation that the wisdom and the love of the church will prevail.

If all three of these steps toward reconciliation fail, then the offender is to be treated as a pagan or tax collector. Jesus did not refuse to speak to them, teach them, touch them or even eat with them. He loved them. Was it His desire that we treat them as though they were never a part of His Kingdom? Are we to start over again to share the love of Christ, to point them to Him?

As leaders in our families, our homes, where we work and play we will personally encounter conflict. Someone will offend and hurt us. We will find ourselves in the position to need to follow these instructions for reconciliation. Opportunities abound to lead fellow believers to resolve conflicts the way Jesus taught us. Leaders help others in their sphere of influence to resolve conflicts.

Your Ministry of Reconciliation and Peacemaking

I want to be known and recognized as a child of God, don't you? Jesus said, "Blessed are the peacemakers, for they will be called sons of God" (Matt. 5:9). As believers, we are God's children because He willfully chose to adopt us into His family. We don't need to be peacemakers to be children of God, but because we are children of God, it is in our DNA to make peace.

If you lead as a parent of more than one child you probably have more experience than you desire as a peacemaker. You may need to end arguments and referee fights all too frequently. You are not alone. I often hear business leaders in management positions lament, "I feel like I am just a glorified babysitter, settling arguments, dealing with dissatisfied employees, and listening to staff whine and cry over such childish things."

To become a successful peacemaker, begin with prayer. Pray for peace where you lead. Regularly prayer-walk your home, property, school, business or territory. Wherever God has given you authority, intentionally, frequently, earnestly and urgently pray for peace. God will reward the time you spend with Him.

To be a successful peacemaker, you must set the example as you live at peace with others. "If it is possible, as far as it depends on you, live at peace with everyone" (Rom. 12:18). It is vital that leaders be very intentional about living peacefully. "Let us therefore make every effort to do what leads to peace and to mutual edification" (Rom. 14:19). Peace is a gift, but a gift we must carefully steward.

Successful peacemakers carry peace wherever they go. Jesus is the Prince of Peace. The kingdom of God is full of peace that surpasses human comprehension. It is God's desire to bring heaven's culture of peace to our world filled with fear, chaos, fighting and war. You represent the Prince of Peace wherever you go. As a royal ambassador of the Kingdom of God, you have access to peace that passes understanding every moment of every day.

I did not begin to grasp the truth that Christians can carry peace until I had been in ministry for several years and I was serving as pastor of a small country church. The leadership of the church held monthly meetings to discuss ministry and to make decisions concerning the life of the church.

One of the leaders came to me after our third session and declared, "Our meetings are really different since you came to be our pastor. Before, there were always loud and long arguments. The last meeting two of our leaders were quarreling and almost got into a fistfight in the church." God began to show me how leaders could carry peace, even though we may be unaware of the power of this gift in us.

Later in my life, God sent me for a season to work outside the church in the marketplace. His assignment was to be an ambassador for His kingdom in the company. I soon learned the staff had bickered and frequently argued over the last several months. The tension level in staff meetings often escalated to yelling and some of the staff nearly coming to physical blows. God revealed His desire to bring peace to this company of believers and nonbelievers.

I arrived a few minutes early my first day of work to prayer walk the property, specifically asking God to bring His peace. The very first minutes as an employee I had the opportunity to pray with a member of the staff whose close friend had been in a near-fatal car accident the previous day. I watched God's peace lift her countenance immediately as we prayed. As spiritual leaders, we are to be known for our peacemaking abilities.

I walked the property boundaries and faithfully prayed for peace most every day I worked. While employed by the company, I never witnessed any arguments, raised voices or a high level of conflict within the staff.

Spiritual leaders are called to partner with God to end division and conflict among the people we lead. God has also invited and challenged us to minister reconciliation between the people we lead and Himself.

> Therefore, if anyone is in Christ, he is a new creation: the old has gone, the new has come! All this is from God, who reconciled us to Himself through Christ and gave us the ministry of reconciliation: that God was reconciling the world to Himself in Christ, not counting men's sins against them. And He has committed to us the message of reconciliation. We are therefore Christ's ambassadors, as though God were making His appeal through us. We implore you on Christ's behalf: Be reconciled to God. (2 Corinthians 5:17-20)

Spiritual leaders have experienced the love of Christ reconciling us to the Father. We live without guilt or shame. Joy fills our hearts as we faithfully repent and consistently enjoy the Father's forgiveness. It is our privilege to represent the King of Kings as His royal ambassadors, bringing the culture of heaven to earth.

Peace on Earth

At the birth of Jesus in Bethlehem His Father in heaven once again announced His plan for peace on earth. The angelic chorus filled the night skies with the song, "Glory to God in the highest, and on earth peace to men on whom His favor rests" (Lk. 2:14).

Our Father sent His Son from heaven to bring peace on the earth. The Prince of Peace represented the King of Kings and revealed how we could experience the peace of heaven. He called and commissioned us, as believers and spiritual leaders to be His ambassadors of peace.

As ambassadors of the Prince of Peace we have the authority and the responsibility to resolve conflict in our own lives and in the lives of others. We are charged with the assignment to bring the culture of heaven to earth.

Heaven is a place of perfect peace. We have the inexplicable experience of His peace reigning in our lives. It is the heart's desire of the Prince of Peace and the King of Kings for peace to envelope the earth and all its inhabitants. You and I have access to peace that passes understanding.

I challenge you to meticulously follow Jesus' practical and effective instructions whenever conflict and offense show their ugly faces in your life. Equip and lead those who follow you to learn and practice the principles the Lord clearly outlined for us. You will be rewarded for your faithful service as an Ambassador for Christ.

You lead. Step up to resolve conflict and prepare the way for the Prince of Peace!

CHAPTER 11: LEADERS EQUIP OTHERS

As the supreme leader of the universe, how does God lead? I believe it is God's nature to partner with human beings to accomplish His goals and plans. He obviously has the power and authority to quickly and effortlessly do everything Himself. He spoke our world and the vast universe into existence. When He speaks, His word has power! He has the authority and dominion to do anything and everything by just speaking it into existence. When He speaks, everything is complete and perfect. He has need of no one and nothing, but He chooses to invite weak, imperfect human beings to partner with Him in what He does. He chose to teach us to walk in His ways and to co-labor with Him.

Jesus came to bring the culture of heaven to earth. Like His Father, He chose not to do it alone. Jesus trained and sent out twelve ambassadors of His kingdom to accomplish this mission. He taught the disciples by first doing His ministry as they watched. Then our Lord gave them the opportunity to do the work of ministry as He watched, advised and corrected them. He finally placed the ministry in their hands with the promise that He would go with them always to the ends of the earth.

God raises up leaders to equip all His ambassadors to fulfill their Kingdom assignments. Ephesians 4:11-13 says,

> It was He who gave some to be apostles, some to be prophets, some to be evangelists, and some to be pastors and teachers, to prepare God's people for works of service, so that the body of Christ may be built up until we all reach unity in the faith and in the knowledge of the Son of God and become mature, attaining to the whole measure of the fullness of Christ.

Leaders Multiply Their Impact

You have a great vision. Your leadership is beginning to make an impact. If you want to see your vision to help God transform our world fulfilled, you must multiply your efforts. Great leaders don't accomplish this by working harder, longer hours. God will increase our impact in His Kingdom as we train, equip, and mentor others. It is imperative that leaders train simply, delegate our authority, impart our gifts and wisdom, and freely release others to lead.

Jesus promised to be with us to the very end of the age. If we desire to be Christ-like, we will not forsake the persons we have mentored in the faith but will maintain contact with them to support, encourage, and correct as necessary.

Train Simply

I learned this lesson from experience with Healing Rooms. As we taught people to pray for healing, we discovered the value of simplicity. We often declared, "This is not rocket science. We are simply praying. We merely communicate with God on behalf of and with other people." We adhered to our version of the K.I.S.S. principle, "Keep It Simple, Saints."

We often make ministry difficult because our training is complicated. Nothing in my experience is more valuable than on-the-job training. We train by telling people why we do things the way we do them. We tell them how we do the things we do. But, nothing equips them quite like on-the-job training. Give them the opportunity to experience it first-hand!

We learn best when both our minds and our hands are actively at work. Take the persons you are training with you as you are involved in ministry. Equip them by allowing them to see you in action. Enable them to observe without stress or pressure to perform. Engage them slowly as the Holy Spirit leads without pressure or stress. It is important to keep a balance between their being prepared and nudging them out of their comfort zone where they watch you do the work or ministry.

Provide the persons you mentor access to the resources that enabled you to succeed. Recommend books, conferences, seminars, websites, etc. that helped you get to where you are now. Introduce them to other successful leaders in your field who are willing to share their wisdom with others.

Delegate Authority

As leaders, we are often tempted to do things ourselves. Our temptation comes from a variety of motivations. We want the job done right, so we think we must do it ourselves. Our desire to "get the job done right" often translates to the truth that we want the work done our way, so we do it ourselves. We have a desire to be recognized and applauded by others, so we do it ourselves. We sometimes believe we are the only person qualified to accomplish a task, so we do it ourselves. We don't think we have the time to train someone else, so we continue to do it ourselves.

Jesus delegated. He shared the love of the Father with the least, the last and the lost. But, our Lord trained, equipped and released the Twelve and then seventy-two others to do the things He was doing. He healed the sick, raised the dead, cleansed lepers, and drove out demons. He gave the disciples the authority to do what He was doing (see Matt. 10:8). Delegating His authority increased significantly the number of people who would experience a supernatural transformation of their lives.

Moses delegated his God-given authority to other leaders. Exodus 18 records how Moses listened to his father-in-law when Jethro encouraged him to delegate his judicial responsibilities to other leaders.

> Moses' father-in-law replied, "What you are doing is not good. You and these people who come to you will only wear yourselves out. The work is too heavy for you; you cannot handle it alone. Listen now to me and I will give you some advice, and may God be with you. You must be the people's representative before God and bring their disputes to Him. Teach them the decrees and laws, and show them the way to live and the duties they are to perform. But select capable men from all the people—men who fear God, trustworthy men who hate dishonest gain—and appoint them as officials over thousands, hundreds, fifties and tens. Have them serve as judges for the people at all times, but have them bring every difficult case to you; the simple cases they can decide themselves. That will make your load lighter, because they will share it with you. If you do this and God so commands, you will be able to stand the strain, and all these people will go home satisfied." (Exodus 18:17-23)

God revealed a definite plan for this work to Jethro. Jethro shared the simple plan with Moses, who wisely adopted God's plan. His work became significantly lighter as many leaders shared the load. Note how Moses was to choose gifted persons with strength of character. He was to train them simply. It would not be easy to put into practice the content of the lessons they needed to learn, but the approach was to be simple. The division of labor was such that no leader would be burdened or overwhelmed with the task.

Impart Your Gifts and Wisdom

Imparting is different from training. We train persons whom we mentor by sharing the practical knowledge we have gained. Impartation, however, is a supernatural, spiritual act. Impartation supernaturally equips the recipients with power and wisdom to fulfill their calling and destiny.

Numbers 11 records one of the early accounts of the experience of impartation. Moses is fed up with all the complaining he endured. This incident is not the first whining and complaining he has heard. This time the people want something besides manna to eat. They want meat and the delicacies they once enjoyed in Egypt. Moses is on the verge of leader burnout. He is ready to relinquish his calling to lead the Israelites.

> I cannot carry all these people by myself; the burden is too heavy for me. If this is how You are going to treat me, put me to death right now—if I have found favor in Your eyes—and do not let me face my own ruin." The Lord said to Moses: "Bring Me seventy of Israel's elders who are known to you as leaders and officials among the people. Have them come to the Tent of Meeting, that they may stand there with you. I will come down and speak with you there, and I will take of the power of the Spirit that is on you and put the Spirit on them. They will help you carry the burden of the people with you so that you will not have to carry it alone. (Numbers 11:14-17)

This biblical story lifts valuable spiritual principles to our attention. First, be proactive, instead of reactive. Moses was exhausted and fearful he would fail. He was tired, and his feelings overwhelmed him. Moses could have requested assistance long before he did. Notice, as soon as he asked, God granted his request.

Second, God gave Moses the responsibility to identify the persons who would receive the impartation. Moses was very well acquainted with the character and gifts of the persons whom he would designate for impartation. He had observed their leadership potential for some time. His decision would be neither arbitrary nor ill-informed.

Finally, it was only God who could take some of the power of the Spirit on Moses and transfer it to the leaders Moses chose. Moses would immediately experience relief from his overwhelming burden.

Release Freely

Micromanaging is counterproductive for any leader. Yes, God is in the details and details matter. Yes, accomplishing the task with excellence matters. Yes, we are ultimately responsible. But, as leaders we cannot fulfill our calling and assignment while micromanaging. Release persons who are gifted and passionate to fulfill their roles and responsibilities.

We want to make certain to accomplish our mission as fully and as accurately as is humanly possible. The temptation is to do it ourselves. "If you want a job done right, do it yourself." Sometimes, this temptation is born out of the misguided desire to control.

Correct Gently

At times, the leaders we mentor and release into leadership will fail. It is our responsibility as leaders to take the lead to admonish and restore them.

God's Word instructs spiritual leaders to correct gently. "Brothers, if someone is caught in a sin, you who are spiritual should restore him gently. But watch yourself, or you also may be tempted" (Gal. 6:1).

I had a recent experience where a leader in authority over me joined one of my peers to question my leadership. Although I had failed to fulfill their expectations, I did not believe I had fallen into sin. At a crossroads when I decided to obey God rather than man I received a letter detailing how I was disobeying the law of the church. I was hurt by the letter outlining potential charges. The letter made me feel like a criminal who had committed a felony. I felt my reputation was being thrown to the dogs. There was probably no intention on their part to elicit my response, but I thought kindness and gentleness were absent from their communication.

As spiritual leaders, we must resist the temptation to write people off who have failed to meet either our understanding of God's desires or our own expectations. It is often a strong human temptation to want to have nothing to do with leaders who have failed. We can, on the other hand, approach people who have failed with love and kindness. It is vital to listen carefully to God to know what to say, what to do, and when to do it.

Encourage Faithfully

In chapter one, "Leaders Love," I lauded the value of expressing love to others through words of affirmation. Let me emphasize how vital it is to encourage the persons whom you mentor.

Your God-given responsibility to mentor is never finished. You will multiply the impact of your life in the Kingdom of God when you train others simply, delegate your authority, impart your gifts and wisdom, release them freely, and correct them gently. But if you only rebuke and correct the persons you mentor they will never reach their full potential. Your constant encouragement will have an incredible impact on their success.

Monitor the persons you mentor to determine when they are bearing fruit. Watch for the ways they use their spiritual gifts. Be aware of times when the people you lead are disheartened. Faithfully encourage them with an email, a text, a note, a phone call, or a word timely spoken face to face.

If God has given you the spiritual gift of encouragement, offering words of affirmation will come easy for you. However, you may need to use your gift more intentionally. Your words carry light and life to everyone around you.

If you do not have the gift of encouragement, begin by asking God to give it to you. Devise a plan to offer encouragement to those you lead. When family members, volunteers or employees simply fulfill their responsibilities, sincerely express your appreciation. When they do something to the best of their ability, let them know.

Your Vision Fulfilled by Others

It may well be that you will be unable to fulfill your dreams in your lifetime. It was true for Moses. He invested over forty years of his life to leading the Israelites to the land God promised to them. But, Moses never lived in the Promised Land. He only caught a very brief glimpse of that vast and beautiful country from the pinnacle of Mount Pisgah. But, the Lord instructed him to mentor Joshua. "But commission Joshua, and encourage and strengthen him, for he will lead this people across and will cause them to inherit the land that you will see" (Deut. 3:28).

As we read the biblical accounts of the life of Joshua we understand how Moses equipped Joshua to lead. He trained simply, delegated his authority, imparted his gifts and wisdom, released Joshua freely, corrected him gently, and encouraged him faithfully.

Moses taught Joshua simply. Joshua watched throughout his life as Moses led the Israelites. From his youth, Joshua is recognized as Moses' aide (see Num. 11:28 and 33:11). He is trained by God and Moses as he accompanies Moses on the mountain to meet and talk with God. Joshua learned to listen to the voice of God and to obey Him.

The first time we meet Joshua in scripture Moses has delegated his authority to Joshua to lead as the commander-in-chief of the Israelite army (see Ex..17:9-13). Moses again reveals the level of trust he has in Joshua when he sends Joshua into the land of Canaan as one of the twelve spies (see Num. 13-14). Here Moses again delegated his authority to Joshua and to the other spies.

God instructed Moses to impart his gifts and wisdom to Joshua in Numbers 27:15-23. God had already given Joshua the gift of leadership. When Moses and Eleazer, the priest laid their hands on Joshua before the entire community, God supernaturally empowered and gifted him to lead the people of Israel.

The same commission and authority given by God to Moses are now granted to Joshua. From this point forward, Joshua's gift of wisdom is seen in the fact that he consults with God whenever any decision needs to be made (see Num. 27:21). The results of this impartation are found in Deuteronomy 34:9, "Now Joshua son of Nun was filled with the spirit of wisdom because Moses had laid his hands on him. So the Israelites listened to him and did what the Lord had commanded Moses."

Moses released and encouraged Joshua to fulfill his destiny as the leader of Israel. In Deuteronomy 31:7-8 we read,

> Then Moses summoned Joshua and said to him in the presence of all Israel, "Be strong and courageous, for you must go with this people

into the land that the Lord swore to their ancestors to give them, and you must divide it among them as their inheritance. The Lord Himself goes before you and will be with you; He will never leave you nor forsake you. Do not be afraid; do not be discouraged."

Train a Team of Ambassadors

God has given spiritual leaders the vision as Ambassadors for Christ to bring His Kingdom to the earth. He intends the culture of heaven to transform the whole earth. He never intended for us to do this alone. He invites us to partner with Him as He calls, equips and commissions teams of Ambassadors for Christ to accomplish His vision. Don't attempt to do it alone. Don't wait until you are near the end of your work and ministry to equip other leaders. Begin today.

You will multiply the impact you make on the Kingdom of God as you train simply, delegate the authority God has given you, partner with God to supernaturally impart your gifts and wisdom, and freely release those whom you have helped to equip. Continue to mentor these leaders as you gently correct and faithful encourage them.

You lead. Step up to equip others!

GARY D. BALL

CHAPTER 12: LEADERS MAKE A DIFFERENCE

You are making a difference, a life-long impact, in someone's life. Yes, you! As you lead, your children's lives dramatically change. When you lead in Christian ministry, your words and actions are influencing the lives of others. Your professional decisions in the marketplace are having a tangible effect on the lives of the people you lead.

I long to make a difference in the lives of others, helping them to have richer, fuller lives—enabling the people I encounter to have a closer walk with Jesus.

It is often difficult for spiritual leaders to envision the results of their efforts. There have been many times in my life when I wondered if I was making any difference at all. There have been times I would have liked to be a building contractor so I could more readily see the results of my work. When a building contractor's team begins, there is nothing but a piece of property. But, as they build they can see the foundation, then the framework and the roof. The windows, doors, drywall, and paint provide visible evidence of their work. A building contractor can readily see the tangible outcome of their efforts.

Sometimes we lead in an arena where it is difficult to know if we are making a difference. As a pastor, I wasn't certain at times my teaching, preaching, pastoral care and leadership were making the kind of difference I desired. But, God showed me something that kept me from being discouraged for extended periods of time.

I learned what I now identify as the "iceberg principle." I discovered only ten percent of an iceberg is visible above the surface of the water. Another "invisible" ninety percent of the iceberg is below the water's surface. God revealed to me that Christian ministry is like the iceberg. We only see a small percentage of the impact our ministry is making. But, unseen below the surface we have made a much larger impression on the lives of people. God has always been faithful to show me enough of the impact of ministry to keep me encouraged.

There have been times as a pastor that the iceberg principle kept me from giving up. While serving as pastor of the Masonville and Utica United Methodist Churches near Owensboro, Kentucky, I did not consider my ministry successful unless people were accepting Christ as their Savior. I wanted my leadership to have eternal consequences in the lives of the people I served.

While there were a few individuals who had made decisions for Christ through the ministry of the larger Masonville United Methodist Church, no one was saved because of the ministry of the Utica United Methodist Church for eighteen months. A few months into that time I began to be discouraged and to ask God, "What am I missing or doing wrong at Utica? I plant the seed and water it, but the ministry is not producing any harvest." I worked faithfully, and I prayed diligently. But, month after month, there were no decisions for Christ that I was aware of. In desperation, I cried out to God.

One Wednesday morning, I made hospital visits before going to the Bible study I led at noon with the Utica congregation. At the Bible study, I learned a woman who lived near the church, whom we had encouraged to come worship with us, was hospitalized.

Although I had already been to the hospital, God emphatically sent me back that afternoon. When I entered the lady's room, her son, whom I had not yet met, was seated on her bed. He looked at me and with excitement in his voice declared, "You are a preacher, aren't you? I have been praying for God to send a pastor here. I need help to know how to get right with Him." I was overjoyed I could help him enter a relationship with God. He did not make the decision that day, but within a few days, he gave his life to Jesus!

The results of planting seeds and watering the soil soon began to produce a harvest. On one Sunday at the end of the eighteen months, I had the awesome opportunity to baptize nine new believers into the faith and life of our little church! So many people joining our small fellowship of fifty made a significant impact. We did not realize that God was at work "below the surface" where we could not see. Our ministry was making a difference in the lives of others!

Maybe you don't believe you are making a difference where you lead. Remember the "iceberg principle." You may only be able to see ten percent of the impact of your leadership on your team. But, you are making a difference and it is much more significant than you can visualize.

Expect God to reveal to you how your leadership is impacting those under your care. Don't expect to learn how you are influencing everyone. Remember the iceberg principle. You are making a difference!

I had another personal experience that helped me see in a very dramatic way that I am making a difference as a leader. I served as senior pastor of the Crestwood United Methodist Church near Louisville, Kentucky for three years. I asked God to guide my steps in the weeks before my first day there as pastor. It became apparent His plan was for our ministry to be focused on prayer and a personal relationship with God through Jesus Christ. I began preaching and teaching on prayer and walking close to God.

Many days I wondered if my leadership was making much difference—disappointed I wasn't making a significant impact on more people's spiritual lives. I desperately tried to be faithful to keep the ministry focused on the priorities God had set.

At the close of three years of ministry in Crestwood God called Marcia and me to be a part of planting a prayer and healing ministry in Madisonville, Kentucky. I despaired when it appeared so little fruit was produced through my leadership at Crestwood. I was beginning to believe God was moving me into a new season of my life in part because I had failed Him in this season. But, my understanding dramatically changed on our last Sunday with the church.

The leaders of the church invited Marcia and me to sit with the congregation during the worship. They wanted us to have front row seats to view a video. We watched the video through tears of thankfulness and joy. The members were asked to answer the question, "How has Pastor Gary and Marcia's ministry impacted your life?" Thirty-two people responded briefly in the seventeen-minute video. We were amazed when person after person expressed their appreciation for helping them grow in their relationship with God and in their prayer life. In fact, eighteen of the thirty-two people on the video shared very articulately how our ministry had helped them to enter a personal relationship with God through prayer!

In the first months of leading the church as senior pastor, God had led us to start a new ministry. Every Sunday believers gathered in a room during both worship experiences to pray for the church and the services. It brought great joy and confidence to have five to seven persons pray with me before the worship service began. They continued in prayer throughout worship interceding for me, the worship leaders, our guests, and the church. Several members in the video spoke of the difference the Prayer Partners Ministry had made in their lives.

We left the church knowing we had made a meaningful difference in the lives of others!

I hope you hear the voice of God today. You are making a difference! Don't give up. Don't be discouraged. Don't listen to the lies of the enemy. Don't allow him to steal your joy. Don't allow him to prevent you from using your God-given gift of leadership to influence others for His Kingdom. Your leadership is making a difference.

GARY D. BALL

You lead. Step up!

ABOUT THE AUTHOR

Gary Ball has served in a wide variety of spiritual leadership positions throughout his adult life, as youth pastor, chaplain of a retirement and nursing home, associate pastor, senior pastor, and pastor to pastors. As senior pastor, he served in churches with as few as twelve and as many as 1,200, sometimes serving multiple churches at one time. God has sent him and his family to ten communities where He demonstrated His favor and gave him the wonderful gift of favor with others for thirty-two years of shepherding His people.

In 2009, God called Gary from pastoral ministry with a local congregation to prayer ministry for community transformation and spiritual awakening.

Happily married to Marcia since 1975, God has shown His unique favor to them with the gifts of three sons and their families. Manuel and Ginny live with their four children in Owensboro, Kentucky. Aaron makes his home in Mills River, North Carolina. Joel and Lacey live in Glasgow, Kentucky with their two daughters.

In 2013, Gary and Marcia returned to the home of their childhood in Mills River, North Carolina to help care for their aging parents. Marcia joyfully serves in ministry as a registered nurse with Hospice. Their ministry in the church and community focuses on prayer, healing, spiritual awakening and community transformation.

Other Books by the Author
A Life of Prayer: Step Closer to God
Available through Amazon, Kindle, and Audible.

Contact the Author
9569 Boylston Highway
Mills River, North Carolina 28759
garydball@att.net

Made in the USA
Columbia, SC
14 December 2017